Café 1

CRÈME

MÉTHODE DE FRANÇAIS

# STUDY GUIDE

## Daphne Jenkins BA

Lecturer in French, Messier-Dowty Ltd, Gloucester
Chief Examiner, French for Business, AEB
formerly Principal Examiner and Reviser, GCSE French, SEG

EUROPEAN
SCHOOLBOOKS
PUBLISHING

All enquiries should be addressed to:
European Schoolbooks Publishing Ltd
The Runnings
Cheltenham GL51 9PQ
England

ISBN 0-85048-101-5

Printed and bound in Great Britain by
Redwood Books, Trowbridge, Wiltshire

# TABLE DES MATIÈRES / Contents

# Préface

Welcome to your Study Guide for **Café Crème**, a new and innovative French course for adult beginners.

**Café Crème** was written and produced in France, by French people. You will already have seen the attractive, very French, lay-out and presentation of the student's book, with its excellent photos and illustrations. You will be hearing recordings of French people and maybe seeing them on the video recordings which accompany the course.

This Study Guide has been prepared to help you make the most of the course. The language spoken by real French people does not always follow simple, strict rules; like English, it has its everyday idioms and expressions, and it reflects and is rooted in the way of life of the French people. The Study Guide explains and clarifies what is in the student's book at every step, and adds much interesting background information. You will never be at a loss to understand. You will be able to consolidate what you have learnt in class, and if you miss a lesson, you will easily be able to make up for it in your own time.

## STRUCTURE OF THE COURSE

**Café Crème** has a very careful plan and structure to justify the inclusion in its title of **Méthode de français** or "Method of learning French."

The student's book is divided into four parts, each dealing with particular language skills:

**Part 1** teaches you to converse, and to make and maintain contact with other French speaking people;

**Part 2** teaches you to express opinions and to argue;

**Part 3** teaches you to understand descriptions and explanations, and to describe and explain yourself, and

**Part 4** teaches you to recount and narrate.

In this Study Guide you will find an introduction to each of the four parts, telling you exactly what to expect about the material covered in the course.

Each of the four parts contains four separate units, dealing with topics, such as greetings, restaurants, health, fashion, work etc. These topics cover all the language needed for day-to-day conversation with French speaking people. Again, page by page notes on each unit in this Study Guide explain and elucidate all the work covered.

Each of the sixteen units is divided into three sections:

1. **DÉCOUVERTES**/Discoveries. In these sections you discover new language by means of documents, texts and recordings and practise this language by various activities and exercises.

2. **BOÎTE À OUTILS**/Toolbox. In these sections you will find a pattern in the language learnt by systematising the grammar and vocabulary introduced.

3. **PAROLES EN LIBERTÉ**/Speaking freely. In these sections you practise using the language learnt in different situations and make it your own. In each of the first three you meet one of a group of four friends who were students together. In the last one, all the friends meet again at the Pyramide du Louvre in Paris.

As each of the four friends lives and works in a different part of France, you will learn about different towns and areas of France, as well as about different jobs and lives.

After every two units there is an extra section, alternately **Bilan** and **Civilisation.**

**BILAN** Revision exercises. These give you a further opportunity to check that you have assimilated and learnt the language covered so far.

## CIVILISATION

These sections describe aspects of French civilisation, the geography of France, life in the cities and countryside, the annual round of festivals, and what to see and do in Paris.

**Café Crème** reflects at every stage the interests, preoccupations and life style of young adults and older people in France today. There are documents about jobs and unemployment, about marriage and divorce, about the changing role of women. One young man is surprised to learn that a girl he first knew as a child is about to become his boss. Jacques, the taxi driver, enjoys listening to reggae music as he drives around.

## LEXIQUE / VOCABULARY LIST

At the back of the Study Guide there is a French-English vocabulary list of the 800 words used in the course. Remember that the first 800 words learnt in a language will probably cover 90% of the words used in the language. There are also verb tables for reference.

## PRONUNCIATION AND INTONATION

As you would expect you are introduced to the French alphabet in Unit 1 and given practice in pronunciation and intonation in each of the sixteen units. These sections are called **Phonétique** and **Mélodies**.

The importance of good pronunciation cannot be exaggerated. Although there are many words which look the same in French and English, such as: **station, intelligence, client, orange, service,** every one of these words is pronounced differently in the two languages. You cannot listen too often to the French speakers and try to reproduce the sounds and rhythms that they produce.

## TEXTS AND DIALOGUES

The texts and dialogues used are carefully graded; they contain only the language being learnt in the unit or the language that has already been learnt in a previous unit. The vocabulary, too, is deliberately restricted so that you get to grips gradually with the most useful and frequently used words in French, without being burdened with more difficult or way-out words.

## ROLE PLAYING

The most important part of a beginner's course is the opportunity to practise using the language being learnt. Right from the start **Café Crème** encourages you to take an active part in the learning process, by question and answer and by repeating and devising role plays.

## THE WORLD OF WORK

You are quickly introduced to telephoning, making appointments, job advertisements and writing formal and informal letters. This material about the world of work is especially useful if you are learning French for use at work.

## HUMOUR

There is plenty of gentle humour in **Café Crème**, both in the illustrations and in the dialogues. The student's interest is also held by the use of cryptic messages and seemingly strange events. **C'est bizarre!**

## SOS GRAMMAIRE

You will find on Page 48 of this Study Guide a summary of grammatical terms just in case you are not familiar with any of the words used in the course. This is followed by a **Précis grammatical,** a summary of all the grammar taught in the book.

## TRANSCRIPT OF THE RECORDINGS

Most of the recorded texts are printed in your textbook, and indicated with a cassette symbol. The few which are not - mainly listening exercises - are printed on page 66 of this study guide.

# BIENVENUE! Welcome!

This first contact with French shows how people greet each other and introduce themselves. It includes some useful classroom words and phrases.

*Page 6*

**Je m'appelle ....** = I am called/ My name is....
**Je suis** = I am.

**Un étudiant** = a male student. **Une étudiante** = a female student.

**Vous vous appelez comment**? = What are you called? What is your name?

**Présentez-vous et dites votre nom** = Introduce yourself and say your name.

**Écoutez** = Listen. **Répétez** = repeat.

*Page 7*

**Vous pouvez répéter, s'il vous plaît?** = Can you repeat, please?

**Lisez** = Read. **Parlez** = Speak. **Regardez** = Look. **Écrivez** = Write.

**Répondez** = Answer.

**Vous avez compris?** = Did you understand?

**Je ne sais pas** = I do not know. **Je ne comprends pas** = I do not understand.

*Page 8*

**PRÉSENTATIONS** = INTRODUCTIONS

## DIALOGUE A

**Kyoko et Thierry sortent de l'université** = Kyoko and Thierry are going out of the university.

**Tu es/ vous êtes** = You are. **J'apprends le français** = I am learning French.

## DIALOGUE B

**J'habite** = I live. **Vrai ou faux**? = True or false? **Exprimez-vous** = Express yourself.

We are briefly introduced to three people whom we are going to meet again in **Paroles en Liberté**, Jacques Mistral, the architect, Martine Cazenave, the café owner, and Joseph, the taxi driver.

**Les mélodies.** The best way to learn correct pronunciation and intonation is to listen carefully to the cassette and then repeat as often as possible what the French people are saying.

# PARTIE 1 **Bonjour...**

*In Part 1 you will learn how to*
- *greet people and introduce yourself to them*
- *give your name, age, and address*
- *talk about what you like and dislike*
- *talk about family, jobs and places of work*
- *ask other people about themselves*
- *make arrangements by telephone for meeting people*
- *talk about the weather and times and dates*
- *use many numbers*

## MEETING AND GREETING PEOPLE FORMALLY

In France people not only shake hands firmly when meeting for the first time but also on every subsequent occasion that they come together and part.

### Monsieur, Madame AND Mademoiselle

It is polite to address everyone to whom you speak as either **Monsieur**, for a man, **Madame,** for a married woman, or **Mademoiselle,** for an unmarried woman**. Madame** is used for an older woman if you do not know whether she is married or not and **Mademoiselle** for a woman who looks too young to be married.

### USING **vous**

In a formal situation, when talking to a stranger or to a person you do not know well you must always address them as **vous** and use the polite forms, such as **Enchanté** and **Comment allez-vous?**

### SURNAME FIRST

When giving their name in a formal situation, such as registering at a hotel, French people often give their surname first and then their first name. For example: **Je m'appelle Guillem... Michel.**

### Bonjour, Bonsoir

**Bonjour** is used when meeting for the first time, to mean *Good morning* or *Good afternoon* or *Hallo*. **Au revoir** means *Goodbye*, but in the evening **Bonsoir** is used to mean both *Hallo* and *Goodbye*.

## MEETING AND GREETING PEOPLE INFORMALLY

When greeting family, friends or young children informally, French people replace the formal handshake by the kiss on the cheek, **la bise** or **le bisou**. According to the region or to individual preference, the number of kisses can vary from one to four. Even men kiss each other in this way, especially within the family. Instead of the more

formal **Bonjour** many people (especially the young) use **Salut!** or **Ça va?** which can be answered just by **Ça va!** or **(très) bien, merci**.

## USING **Tu**

**Tu** is usually used instead of the formal **vous** when speaking to a member of your family, a close friend or a child.

This is not quite so simple as it sounds, as French people often behave for longer in a formal way than English people. It is safer to keep on addressing a French acquaintance as **vous** until such time as s/he feels friendly enough to change to **tu** and say something like **On se tutoie?** or *Shall we use tu?*

Do not be surprised if you discover that there is no absolute rule about the use of **tu** and **vous**. Usage varies according to social class (some aristocratic husbands and wives address each other as **vous**), between generations (most young people use **tu** to each other), and according to the situation, as an indication of emotions such as affection or anger. If an irate French motorist does not approve of someone's driving, s/he is quite likely to jump out of his/her car in order to remonstrate with the offending driver, who will very likely be addressed as **tu**.

## NAMING THE BABY

If you have noticed that French people seem to have a number of first names this is because babies used to be given the name of their father or mother and often the name of their godmother or godfather and perhaps the name of the saint for the day on which the baby was born. Even now, every French baby must by law be given at least two names.

Although the state has been more tolerant in recent years about allowing parents to name their children as they wish, a few years ago a couple were forced to choose a new name for their daughter, whom they had registered as **Prune**. Early in 1997 another couple very keen on sailing is awaiting the ruling of a court in Rouen as to whether they will have to change the name of their newly-born twins, registered as **Bâbord** (Port) and **Tribord** (Starboard).

Even if the child is not named after the saint for his/her birthday s/he will still enjoy his/her **jour de fête** when s/he may receive cards and small presents.

TELEPHONING

As most French people now have the telephone in their homes and the system is extremely efficient, it is useful to learn to speak to people in this way. Although the person who answers the telephone may say **Allô** when s/he picks up the receiver, instead of **Bonjour**, the caller will respond to this by the polite **Bonjour** or **Bonsoir**, followed by the customary **monsieur, madame** or **mademoiselle**.

# UNIT 1 Préférences

**Skills**
- saying what you like and don't like
- asking someone what s/he likes
- **tu** or **vous**

**Grammar**
- making an affirmative and negative statement
- asking questions
- **moi, toi, vous**
- verbs in **- er**
- **je, tu, vous**
- definite articles: **le, la, les**
- plural of nouns

**Vocabulary**
- tastes: sport, shows, transport
- **aimer, préférer**

*Page 10*

1. **J'aime... Je n'aime pas...** I like/love... I don't like/love.

As French vocabulary is not always as rich as English vocabulary, one word in French sometimes has to serve for two words in English. This is the case with the verb **aimer**, which means both to like and to love. One way of making it clear that you are especially fond of something is to use the verb **adorer** = to adore.

In this rhyming song **Eléonore** rhymes with **aéroports** as the two final consonants of **aéroports** are not pronounced, **cafés** rhymes with **mai** as the final **s** of **cafés** is not pronounced and **Arthur** rhymes with **peinture**.

**Je** becomes **J'** before a vowel (**J'aime**) and **ne** becomes **n'** before a vowel (**je n'aime pas**).

**Repérez les mots que vous connaissez.** Pick out the words that you know.

*Page 11*

2. **Vous aimez** = you like. The parts of the verb **aimer** change, as shown on p.14.

2. **Toi, moi** and **vous** are pronouns used for extra emphasis. **Moi, j'aime la musique** = *I* like music. **Tu aimes la musique, toi?** = Do *you* like music?

In the field of modern pop music France, like many other countries, imports much from America and from Britain. The French solo artists and groups struggling to establish themselves have been helped by the government which has recently decreed that at least a third of the music played on the radio must be French.

*Page 12*

3. **GÉNIAL!** Fantastic! / Great! / Brilliant!

**Génial, beau, bizarre, magnifique** and **terrible** are all adjectives used to describe the work of art shown in the picture. In this context **terrible** means "terrible" but the word is also used to mean "terrific" or "tremendous", as in **C'était une soirée terrible**.

6. Look carefully and say what you think.

**C'est** = It is. **Ce n'est pas** = It is not.

4. **Portraits** The tennis player is Yannick Noah; the actress is Juliette Binoche and the sailor and environmentalist is Jacques Cousteau, who died in 1997. **J'aime danser** = I like to dance *or* I like dancing. **J'aime voyager** = I like to travel *or* I like travelling.

7. Who is speaking? Match the text and the photo.

8. Think of a famous person.

Read the text again and write one of your own.

*Page 13*

2. **La marche** = walking. **Le foot** = football. **Le vélo** = cycling.

You will notice that most of the words for sports in this unit look very much like English ones: **le judo, le tennis, la boxe, le foot(ball), la danse**. This is because the French have, in fact, imported many games from England. It was the British Tommies in the first world war who first introduced the game of rugby football to the South of France.

Although **le tennis** sounds very like the English game of tennis, tennis has, in fact, been developed from the old French **jeu de paume**, played in a large hall with a gallery, by striking a ball with the palm of the hand.

**Le vélo** or cycling, competes with football for being the most popular sport in France. The annual cycle race, **Le Tour de France**, is thought by many to be the most demanding sporting event in the world and is followed every summer by millions of enthusiastic fans.

THE ALPHABET. It is very useful indeed to learn to recite the French alphabet. This will help you to pronounce letters correctly and also to spell out words and to understand acronyms or sets of initials like **Le R.E.R.** = **le réseau express régional** (suburban underground) or **L'U.E.** = **L'Union Européenne** (the European Union).

Listen carefully to the sound of the **accent aigu** or acute accent and learn to distinguish it from the **accent grave** or grave accent. The **accent circonflexe** or circumflex

9

usually lengthens a vowel and indicates that there was once an **s** in the original Latin word - (example - **fête** from *festa* or **tête** from the vulgar Latin *testa)*. When it is placed over an **e** it is pronounced like a grave accent.

*Page 14*

## GRAMMAIRE

Check with **SOS Grammaire** if you are uncertain of any grammatical terms used.

**Chassez l'intrus** = Find the odd one out.

## CONJUGAISON: LES VERBES EN -ER.

About two thirds of French verbs belong to the first conjugation, that is, verbs whose infinitive ends in -er, like **aimer**, **regarder** and **danser**. When you look up a verb in the dictionary it is the infinitive you will find, the equivalent of "to like, to look, to dance". The verb forms change according to the person doing the action. Hence, **j'aime** = I like but **tu aimes** = you like (to a person you know well) and **vous aimez** = you like (for a more formal relationship or more than one person). The infinitive of "to prefer" is **préférer** but when the ending of the verb form is silent, the second accent changes from an acute to a grave - **vous préférez** but **je préfère**.

## LA NÉGATION / THE NEGATIVE

To make a statement negative place **ne** or **n'** before the verb and **pas** after the verb. **J'aime > Je n'aime pas** and **C'est > Ce n'est pas.**

## L'INTERROGATION / ASKING QUESTIONS

Affirmation is making a statement, saying that something is so. A statement can be made into a question by changing the intonation, by raising the voice at the end of the sentence or by using the question form **est-ce que ...?**

*Page 15*

**Le nom** = the noun

The definite article **le** is used with a masculine noun (**le soleil**), **la** with a feminine noun (**la peinture**) and **les** with a plural noun (**les aéroports**). **L'** is used with any singular noun that begins with a vowel (**l'école**).

Sometimes the definite article is used in French where it is omitted in English. **J'aime le jazz** = I like jazz, meaning all kinds of jazz and not just one specific kind.

*Pages 16 and 17*

## BIZARRE!

The dialogue on page 16 contains many words and expressions that you have already learnt in this unit, but there are a few additions like **le courrier** = the mail, **salut!** = hi!, hallo, **Hein!** = What?, **jouer** = to play or to act or to gamble and **À bientôt** = See you soon! The dialogue is odd or **bizarre** because Jacques cannot understand why anyone should ask him if he still likes playing / acting / gambling. Jacques is the first of the characters in **Paroles en Liberté** to receive a mysterious message. Watch out for more later!

**Vrai ou faux** = True or false

**Les rythmes et les mélodies** give valuable practice with pronunciation and intonation, with the voice going up for a question and down for a statement. Practice is given too with the even, regular stress given to words of more than one syllable. In English we stress one of the syllables more than the others.

**Exprimez-vous** / Express yourself.

7. **À deux** = in pairs. Here **jouer** means "to act". Here is your chance to take part in role playing, practising much that has been learnt in the unit. It is a good idea to take it in turns to play the different parts.

8. This time you have to prepare the questions and answers yourself before the role play. If you find this easy you could change the questions and answers a little, so that you practise other words as well. For example, you could say that Jacques prefers jazz rather than opera or that he hates dancing.

9. This activity would be enjoyable if students were divided into groups of four or more. Once everyone has written down a list of likes and dislikes, the lists can be moved around and guesses made as to who is responsible for each.

# UNIT 2 **Portraits**

**Skills**
- giving your name, your nationality and your job
- asking someone about his/her identity
- filling in a form

**Grammar**
- asking questions
- the verb **être** with an adjective of nationality
- **être** + name of job
- conjugation of **être** and **-er** verbs
- indefinite articles, **un, une** and **des**

**Vocabulary**
- names of jobs and places of work
- adjectives of nationality
- numbers and figures

*Page 18*

ATHLETICS

We are told that three thousand runners in the marathon come from all over the world and from all walks of life.

All large towns and most small towns and villages as well have a **Stade municipal** or local stadium with a running track, where budding champions can train. Olympic gold medallists like Marie-Jo Pérec encourage youngsters to emulate their considerable achievements in world events.

1. The reporter is excited so he uses words and phrases like **Attention**! = Look! **Oh là là!** = Fancy that! **Formidable** = Wonderful! **Bravo!** = Well done!

JOBS

In this unit we are introduced to a woman pilot and to a male nurse. It is true, of course, that women are now doing many jobs that used to be reserved almost exclusively for men and vice versa. Half of France's doctors are women and France, like England, has had a woman prime minister (Edith Cresson) in recent years. Yet so far there has been no female President of France and there are, currently, very few women **députés** in the National Assembly and not a great many who hold top jobs in industry and trade.

There is more than one way of asking about someone's job. The way that the reporter uses here is **Qu'est-ce que vous faites dans la vie?** = What do you do in life?

Note that French does not use the indefinite article when stating a profession. **Je suis pilote** = I am a pilot.

2. **Faites parler J. Lapierre et F. Dumas** = Find the words that J. Lapierre and F. Dumas would say.

*Page 19*

2. Learn to pronounce clearly all the numbers on this page and make sure that you know them by heart. An accurate knowledge of numbers is essential when expressing yourself and understanding French.

Note especially that **cent** = a or one hundred and **mille** = a or one thousand and also that **deux cents** has a final **s**, whereas in English we say "two hundred, three hundred etc."

6. **Un nombre manque** = A number is missing

*Page 20*

INFORMATION TECHNOLOGY

As computers play a very considerable part in French life today, it is not surprising that some of the runners in the race work in this field (**informaticien** = computer scientist).

3. **Classement** = Placings, final positions. **Classement** can also mean grading or rating in a sport. In tennis, for example, competitions are held so that the best local or national players can be graded according to their ability.

**Ils habitent, ils travaillent** = They live, they work. Note the ending of the verb -**ent** and that the three letters are not pronounced.

*Page 21*

COUNTRIES AND NATIONALITIES

Unlike English, French uses the definite article when naming a country. Hence, **Vive la France.** A few of the countries listed are of masculine gender - **Le Japon, Le Portugal** and **Le Canada** - but most are feminine.

1. Although English uses a capital letter to denote nationality, as in "She is Japanese," French uses a small letter for this, **Elle est japonaise**.

Although most of the adjectives of nationality add an **-e** for the feminine form (japonais = **japonaise**), note that an adjective that already ends in **e** (**suisse**) does not add another **e**. Note also that the adjectives ending in **-en** add **-ne** for the feminine and that **grec** becomes **grecque** in the feminine.

3. When you address someone as **tu** "you are" = **tu es**, but when you use **vous,** "you are" = **vous êtes**.

5. **La fiche d'inscription** = Registration form

French people spend a great deal of their time filling in forms and many complain loudly about bureaucracy.

**Prénom** = First name. **Nom (de famille)** = surname.

## L'INTERROGATION

In speech, if not in writing, it is perfectly acceptable to place the question word **Où?** or **Comment?** at the end of the sentence instead of the beginning, as in **Tu habites où?** or **Vous vous appelez comment?**

## CONJUGAISON: LE VERBE ÊTRE

Note that the verb can be used with nouns (**Elle est étudiante**) as well as with adjectives (**Elle est grecque**).

Make sure that you learn this verb by heart and that you also know all the endings of the **-er** verbs. The **indicatif présent** = the present indicative. This just means that the action of the verb is taking place in the present or now.

## L'ARTICLE INDÉFINI

The indefinite article has two singular forms, **un** = a / one with a masculine noun and **une** with a feminine noun. The plural form **des** = some is included in French where it is often omitted in English, e.g. **Il y a des étudiants à l'université** = There are students in the university.

4. Some nouns denoting a profession add **-e** for the feminine form (**étudiant** > **étudiante**), those ending in **-er** change the **-er** to **-ère**, (**ouvrier** > **ouvrière**), some of those ending in **-eur** change the **-eur** to **-euse**, (**serveur** > **serveuse**) and others change **-eur** to **-rice**, (**acteur** > **actrice**). Whereas nouns ending in **-ien** add **-ne** for the feminine, (**informaticien** > **informaticienne**), those ending in **-e** in the masculine retain the same form in the feminine, (**pilote**).

## UNIVERSITY

Universities in France do not select students in the same way as British universities. Anyone who has passed the **Baccalauréat**, the French equivalent of our A level examination, has the right to register (**s'inscrire**) for a degree course. Most students register at a local university and continue to live at home with their parents.

Often lecture rooms are overcrowded and students do not receive much personal tuition. Neither is there a great deal of help available in the form of scholarships and grants. It is not surprising that a large number of students give up and drop out of their course before taking their final examinations.

## DIALOGUE A

**jour d'inscription** = registration day; **aujourd'hui** = today; **un ordinateur** = a computer.

**toujours** sometimes means "always" but in this context it has the meaning of "still."

## DIALOGUE B

**À la terrasse** = on the terrace; **Il rencontre** = he meets; **La fac** is an abbreviation for **La faculté**. French people, especially young ones, abbreviate many words, such as, **sympa** for **sympathique**, **le bac** or **le bachot** for **le baccalauréat** and **le resto** for **le restaurant**. **L'informatique** = information technology; **Un stage** = a course. There are very many families of words. The verb **étudier** = to study, the noun **étudiant(e)** = student and the noun **études** = studies. If you know one of the words in a family, you will probably be able to guess the meaning of the others.

4. **L'accent tonique** = the stress. Note carefully how the stress moves according to the position of a word in a sentence.

5. When the question word comes at the end of the sentence, the voice rises, but when it comes at the beginning, the voice goes down. When the answer to a question must be yes or no the voice rises.

7. As in England many leisure centres (**centres de loisirs**) have been opened in recent years.

8. **Rédigez** = write, compose. In this family of words you will find **le rédacteur** = the editor and **la rédaction** = writing or editorial staff.

9. Gérard Depardieu and Juliette Binoche are famous French actors. Although Gérard Depardieu has been to Hollywood and acted in such films as *Green Card*, he is more at home when speaking French in such box office successes as **Cyrano de Bergerac** or **Manon des Sources**.

The cinema has always been popular in France where it is known as **le septième art**. It is subsidised by the government and much frequented. A recent film called **Microcosmos** about insect life attracted more than a million cinema goers in the first fortnight after its release.

# UNIT 3 Moi et les autres

**Skills**
- greeting people and introducing them to each other
- giving and asking about age
- talking about the weather

**Grammar**
- the verb **avoir**
- the possessive adjectives
- the preposition **de** + the definite articles
- asking questions with **qui?** and **qui est-ce?**
- C'est

**Vocabulary**
- greetings
- days of the week
- seasons
- months
- numbers
- the family

*Page 28*

### FÊTE

The French have a great capacity for enjoying themselves and a **fête** is a means of doing this. It can be a religious occasion, when there is a national holiday to celebrate Christmas or Ascension Day, or it can be almost any kind of civil occasion as well, from the **Fête nationale** on the 14 July, when the French celebrate the taking of the prison of the Bastille, marking the beginning of the Revolution and the birth of the Republic to a relatively small gathering of people who celebrate with music, dancing, eating, drinking or any other kind of fun and entertainment.

**Tu es seul?** = Are you on your own?

**Il fait beau et chaud**. **Il fait** is the expression to remember and use for describing the weather. Note that although English says "It is fine," French is using the verb **faire** = to do or to make, and not the verb **être** = to be.

*Page 29*

Although we say "I *am* hungry, thirsty, cold or hot" and "I *am* 20 (years old)," French uses the verb **avoir** = to have, rather than **être** = to be, for all these expressions.

Note that the plural of **c'est** is **ce sont**.

**Réécoutez** = listen again. The prefix **re** is placed at the front of many French words to give the meaning of *again*. Hence you could find **relisez** = read again or **redemandez** = ask again.

*Page 30*

### DATES

You will realise that dates are not formed with the same kind of numbers in French as in English. Apart from using the word for the first (**le premier**) for the first day of the month, French uses the cardinal numbers - two, three, four etc., whereas English uses the ordinal numbers, second, third, fourth etc. Also, when we say or write the date in English, we put "Tuesday, the 5th September" or "Friday, the 4 March." This is also the usual way of giving the date in French - "**mardi, le sept septembre**" and "**vendredi, le quatre mars**."

However, French people sometimes prefer to change the position of the day of the week, saying **le mardi, cinq septembre** or **le vendredi, quatre mars**.

Both the days of the week and the months of the year are normally written with a small letter in French, whereas we write them with a capital letter. As there is so much correspondence in English for business these days, you may see a French business letter using a capital letter for a day or a month. This would be tolerated by the **Académie française**, the august body which endeavours to ensure the correct use of the French language.

It is interesting to note that, as French is a Romance language, that is, one directly derived from Latin, and that English is also partly derived from Latin, the days of the week, even if they look and sound very different, have a great deal in common. The **di** that appears in all the French words is derived from the Latin **dies**, which also gave the English word **day**. **Lundi** is the day of the moon, **mardi** is the day of Mars, the God of war, **mercredi** is the day of Mercury, the messenger of the gods, and so on.

### LA MÉTÉO - WEATHER FORECASTING

In a country as large as France and with such geographical variety, weather forecasting can be very important. The regional differences are such that the map on this page gives a temperature of 15 degrees for Lille in the north and of 31 degrees for Toulouse in the south, on the same day. As in Great Britain the press, radio and television all give frequent weather reports and forecasts.

**Chers auditeurs** = Dear listeners. The weather forecast is being given on the radio.

**LE TEMPS** = the weather. **Le temps** is the normal word for the weather but it also has the meaning of time - time in the sense of the passing of time, NOT time by the clock. **Quel temps fait-il?** = What is the weather like? and **Quelle heure est-il?** = What time is it?

Just in case you are not sure about all the weather symbols, here are the meanings of the French words: **Ensoleillé** = sunny, **Éclaircies** = bright periods,

**Nuageux** = cloudy, **Couvert** = overcast, **Averses** = showers, **Pluies** = rain, and **Orage** = thunderstorm.

**Août**. Listen very carefully to the pronunciation of this word. From a word of three syllables in Latin, *agostum*, the French word has been reduced to one syllable and often just a single sound. It is for this reason that many French people prefer to pronounce the final **t**.

You will notice that most compound numbers are separated by a hyphen - **dix-sept** or **vingt-trois** but that **vingt et un** and **trente et un** do not have a hyphen as they have the word **et** instead.

### Page 31

Although many family units may not be as close as they used to be in France - the French are currently marrying less than any other Europeans - the family remains very important in France. We have already noted that French students mostly live at home whilst attending the university. Other young people often remain in the parental home until their late twenties. Those who marry or cohabit do so at a later age than they used to.

Many who do marry will divorce and many wives go on working after marriage so that the average number of children born to a French couple today is not quite two.

It is obvious that the French are making up their own minds on divorce, family planning and abortion, and that many no longer follow the strict ruling of the Catholic church on these family matters.

Notice the hyphen in **grands-parents** which tells us that the word means "grandparents" and not "large parents."

As there is no apostrophe + s to denote possession in French, "Mathilde's brother" has to be expressed by **le frère de Mathilde** = (literally) the brother of Mathilde.

Notice that **son, sa** and **ses** mean both **his** and **her**. **Son** is used before a singular masculine noun (**son mari**) or a singular feminine noun beginning with a vowel (**son amie**) and **ses** is used before any plural noun - **ses collègues, ses soeurs**.

### Page 32

The rules for the agreement of the possessive adjectives **mon, ma** and **mes, ton, ta** and **tes** are the same as those for **son, sa** and **ses**.

Notice that although the final **-ent** on the **ils/elles** form of the verbs in **-er** is not pronounced, the **-ont** with the **ils/elles** of the verb **avoir** is pronounced.

### Page 33

When the preposition **de** comes before the definite article **le**, the two words join together to form **du** (**l'âge moyen du mariage**). **De** also joins with **les** to form **des** (**le père des enfants**), but **de** + **la** remain the same (**la fête de la musique**) as does **de** + **l'** - le frère **de l' infirmier**.

**C'est** can be used before a noun, **C'est une belle ville** and also before an adjective, **C'est formidable!**

### Page 34

Although **une conférence** can mean "a meeting or conference" it can also mean "a lecture" or "talk" as it does here.

**québécoise** is the adjective used to describe an inhabitant of Quebec, the French speaking town and province in Canada. Laval is a town west of Montreal in the province of Quebec.

In 1995 the inhabitants voted for the second time on a referendum to separate Quebec from Canada. Although the referendum was narrowly defeated, there remains a very strong separatist movement in Quebec, where French is spoken with a very distinctive accent and vocabulary, reflecting the influence of the seventeenth century French spoken by the early settlers in Canada and the influence of the English and American spoken in Canada and the United-States.

Annie says **Je connais un petit restaurant** for "I know a small restaurant." You are already familiar with **Je ne sais pas** = I do not know, from the verb **savoir**.

**Savoir** usually means knowing a fact, whereas **connaître** means to know a person or a place, to be acquainted with.

### Page 35

**Les mélodies**

5. Both in a statement and when the question word is placed at the beginning of the sentence, the voice goes down.

# UNIT 4 Carnet d'adresses

**Skills**
- telephoning to make an appointment, to arrange the time and place
- asking for and giving an address

**Grammar**
- possessive adjectives
- questions with **où** and **quand**
- preposition **à** + definite article (**au, à l', à la, aux**)
- imperative of **-er** verbs
- verbs **aller** and prendre

**Vocabulary**
- words for telling the time
- parts of the day

*Page 36*

TELEPHONING

The French telephone system is highly efficient and is now one of the best in the world.

There are so many subscribers that, since the end of 1996, every telephone number in France has been composed of ten figures, the first two being the numbers of one of the five regions. The area around Paris has number 01, North-West France is 02, the North-East is 03, the South-East is 04 and the South-West is 05.

Many retail outlets sell FRANCE TELECOM's **télécarte** (telecard). This is easy to use, as clear instructions are given on all public telephones. Millions of subscribers pay to have access to the thousands of services provided by the MINITEL. Amongst the most useful of these are speedy access to telephone numbers of subscribers anywhere in France, to the services of local trades people, the booking of theatre or cinema seats, telephone shopping and so on.

**Un coup de téléphone** = a telephone call. Other ways of saying this are **un coup de fil** or **un appel (téléphonique)**.

**Allô** is only used by a person answering the telephone, so is not an alternative greeting in other situations. **Bonjour** is, in fact, often used as a greeting on the telephone.

The grave accent on **où?** = where? serves to distinguish it from **ou** meaning "or", just as the accent on **à** = in, at or to (**à Lyon, à Paris**) distinguishes it from **a** meaning "has".

Notice the spelling of the city **Lyon** which is given a final "s" in English.

When Martine says **Je cherche un hôtel**, she means "I am looking for a hotel". As there is no equivalent of the English present continuous in French, **Je cherche** can mean "I look for", "I am looking for" or "I do look for".

FESTIVAL

France, like England, has many cultural festivals, festivals of music, dancing and literature. Notable examples are the annual film festival at Cannes and the festival of theatre and dance at Avignon.

*Page 37*

**à la maison** can mean "at the house" but usually, as here, it means "at home".

ADDRESSES

Notice that **rue, quai, place** etc. used in addresses have a small letter in French, whereas **road, square** etc. are written with a capital letter in English. Note too the spelling differences in **adresse** (one "d") and **appartement** (two "p"s) whereas **address** has two "d"s in English and **apartment** has only one "p".

**Une place** is a square and not a place but **un square** is a garden in the middle of a square.

Be very careful not to confuse **à droite** = to/on the right with **tout droit** = straight on.

Whereas we say "I live at number 80" French includes the definite article, saying **J'habite au numéro 80**.

*Page 38*

3. LETTERS

French people usually write their name and address on the back of the envelope and just write the town and date at the top of their letter.

Note that "Dear" has a masculine form **cher** and a feminine form **chère. Bises** and **Amitiés** are both friendly ways of ending a letter to a friend or relative.

**La gare du Nord** is one of the main line railway stations in Paris. The **arrivées** is the part of the station where the trains come in and the **sortie** is the way out

4. **Je voudrais** = "I would like" is a polite way of saying what you want.

*Page 39*

TELLING THE TIME

French people, like English people, can choose to tell the time by using either the 12 hour clock or the 24 hour clock. However, in France the 24 hour clock is always used for timetables to avoid any possible confusion.

15

The answer to **Quelle heure est-il?** is always **Il est....** as **c'est** is never used when giving the time.

Just as we say "o'clock" for "of the clock" French says **du matin**, **de l'après-midi** and **du soir** for "in the morning" etc.

Notice the way that addresses are written with the post code preceding the name of the town and note, too, the abbreviations for **Monsieur (M.)** and for **Madame (Mme)**.

*Page 40*

You will see that **à** + the definite article behaves like **de** + the definite article.

IMPERATIVE There are only 2 forms of the imperative or command form in English, 'listen' or 'let us listen', but French needs a third form to correspond to the use of **tu.** Notice, however, that the **s** of **tu téléphones** is not used in the command form **téléphone**.

**Aller** and **Prendre.** Notice the different uses of these verbs in French. Although **aller** means "to go" it has the meaning of "to be" in expressions like **je vais bien** = I am well or **ça va** = all is well. **Prendre** can mean "to take" or "to catch" as in **Je prends le train**, but it has the meaning of "to go" in **je prends à droite** and of "to have" in **je prends un café crème.**

*Page 41*

Note that **notre** = our and **votre** = your are used before both a masculine and a feminine singular noun. Remember that **notre** begins with "n" like **nous** and **votre** begins with "v" like **vous.**

*Page 42*

**DIALOGUE A**

Although English usually says *in* the square, French says **sur la place. Oh là là!** The grave accent on **là** distinguishes it from the definite article **la**. When Kyoko says **on est bien** she is using the indefinite pronoun **on** to mean 'we'. French people do this a great deal. **Bien** in this sentence means "comfortable/at our ease". **Nul(le)** means not any, no, but when Thierry says to Kyoko **Tu es nulle**, he means "You are useless/ hopeless".

**DIALOGUE B.**

**Le nouveau centre culturel.** The most famous cultural centre in France is the **Centre national d'art et de culture Georges Pompidou** which was built twenty years ago in the centre of Paris and welcomes more visitors than any other building in the capital. Many visitors go to see the revolutionary design of the building, with its network of pipes outside the building rather than hidden inside. The wear and tear on the building has been such that it closed in 1997 for two years for repairs and refurbishing. When the writer André Malraux was Minister of Culture he created regional cultural centres,

called **Maisons de la culture**, in the hope of taking culture to everyone in France. This venture was not altogether successful and there are now only about ten **Maisons de la culture** in France.

**Le T.G.V.** or **train à grande vitesse**. Since the appearance of the first T.G.V. in 1981 the high speed trains have performed outstandingly well and currently hold the world speed record of 270 km per hour for passenger trains.

*Page 43*

The many cinemas in Paris show both French and foreign films. Philippe Noiret is a well-known French actor.

ESPACES

*Page 44*

The first of the civilisation sections, **Espaces**, deals with the geography of France and its overseas territories, such as **Guadeloupe** and **Réunion**, pictured on this page.

Many of the words used in this section are similar to English words, like **hexagone** (hexagon), **climat** (climate), **varié** (varied) etc.

The map of France shows **les montagnes** (the mountains), **les fleuves** (the main rivers) and reference is made to **le paysage** (the landscape) and to some trees: **le hêtre** = the beech, **le pin maritime** = the maritime pine, **le cyprès** = the cypress and **l'olivier** = the olive tree.

*Page 45*

Most of the words to do with climate found on this page also look rather like English words but **doux** means "mild", **la pluie** = rain and **la neige** = snow.

PHOTOS

1.**La Sainte Victoire** is a small range of mountains to the east of Aix-en-Provence. It was a favourite subject of the painter, Cézanne.

2.**Les Landes** is a region in the south-west of France, on the Atlantic coast. Since the seventeenth century the dry, sandy land has been transformed by the planting of a million hectares of pines, making the area the largest forest in Europe.

*Page 46*

**Les paysages** = the landscapes

**Mon pays, ton pays**. Although **un pays** = a country, the word also has the meaning of "area" or "region" as in **Le pays d'Auge** mentioned on this page. **La campagne** means "the countryside" as opposed to the seaside.

**Une station de ski** = a ski resort.

# PARTIE 2 À mon avis...

*In Part 2 you will learn how to*
- *talk and give opinions about food and drink*
- *order and pay for food in a restaurant*
- *invite people to your home*
- *talk about health, fitness and sport*
- *find your way around a large shop*
- *choose colours and buy clothes*
- *travel by train*
- *talk about holiday preferences and activities*
- *use expressions of quality and time*

## FOOD AND DRINK

Food and drink has and still does play a very important part in French life. Whenever there is an opportunity, whether it be a public holiday or a family celebration the French will meet together over a good meal and good wine. In the case of a wedding feast or a Christmas or New Year dinner, the meal could last for several hours, interspersed with much conversation or even dancing.

Although the pattern of life is changing, with more and more women pursuing a career and with the advent of frozen and convenience food to compensate for time that was formerly spent in the kitchen, most people are very interested in what they eat and drink, both at home and in restaurants. There is a new awareness and pleasure in foreign cooking, with Chinese, Indian, Vietnamese, Italian, Greek, American and even English restaurants and pubs opening everywhere in France. These have come to join the numerous French establishments, ranging from top restaurants, to café-restaurants, brasseries, bistrots, auberges, estaminets, relais routiers to simple bars and self service cafés.

Even if many small cafes are closing, especially in Paris, eating and drinking out are still very popular. Children and even family pets are usually welcome in restaurants, so that the whole family can go out for a meal together. Being a waiter or a waitress is not perceived as a subservient job or one that is just suitable for part-time or student employment, but is often seen as a satisfying worthwhile job. Just as table manners differ in France and England because of different eating habits, so do some of the formalities and conventions concerned with home entertainment. It is usual to take a gift of flowers or wine or a cake to one's host or hostess. If the gift is specially wrapped for the occasion, the host or hostess will open it immediately in order to show appreciation and thank the giver.

## SPORT AND FITNESS

Every French child physically able to do so has to take part in sporting activities at school and pass a leaving examination in sport. There are sports such as handball and volleyball as well as football, athletics, swimming, tennis and basketball. Cycling, fishing and horseriding are also popular and there are plenty of fitness clubs and gymnasiums for aerobics, bodybuilding and other such activities.

## HEALTH

We are told that the French spend an average of 1,000 francs a month on their health care, more than any other Europeans and that only the Americans and Canadians spend more than this. Health is, indeed, a national preoccupation. Employers and employees pay large sums of money to ensure excellent medical services. Instead of being registered with one medical practice only, a French person can consult any doctor or number of doctors that (s)he chooses, about any illness. Social Security reimburses about two thirds of the cost of consultations and medicines and most people have extra private insurance to cover the remaining costs.

The Social Security will even pay for people to go away from home for a health cure (**une cure**) in such special resorts as Aix-les-Bains in south-east France or La Bourboule in the Massif Central. The government, struggling to reduce the national deficit in order to enter the European Monetary System, is attempting to reduce the money it pays out for health but is meeting stiff opposition from people used to enjoying such generous benefits.

## CLOTHES AND SHOPPING

Paris, with its great fashion houses, has long been a centre of **la haute couture** or top fashion. Although the top fashion designers sell most of their clothes to just a few of the world's richest women, the influence of Paris fashion on dress design is enormous and therefore important to France's prestige and prosperity.

Students from all over the world rush to the Paris collections and await with great interest the latest creations of the designers of such houses as Dior, Givenchy and Pierre Cardin. It is interesting to note the success in recent years of young British designers like John Galliano (born in Gibraltar but brought up in London) who became chief designer for Givenchy and in 1996 changed his allegiance to the house of Dior.

Large stores, including recent arrivals like Marks and Spencer and C & A and small shops, too, now sell a range of ready-to-wear clothes. There are also many successful mail order companies such as La Redoute, which offer many reasonably priced clothes, and most shops sell off their surplus stock in sales.

TRAVEL AND HOLIDAYS

The heavily subsidised S.N.C.F. (**Société Nationale des Chemins de fer Français**) provides an excellent rail service in France. New tracks have been built for the high speed T.G.V. and most trains are punctual. There are many special services such as Auto-Rail for transporting cars, and there are very many concessions for all kinds of people, from babies, to students and old people.

A family can travel cheaply by rail to its annual holiday destination.

By law every employee in France is entitled to five weeks paid holiday a year as well as public holidays and extra days off for long service, family bereavement, weddings, births etc. Holidays are eagerly awaited and spent in many different ways, at home or staying with relatives, in the mountains, in the country or at the sea, in hotels, boarding houses or one of the many well-equipped camping and caravanning sites. Activities of all kinds are available to satisfy the army of French and foreign holidaymakers.

# UNIT 5 La pause de midi

**Skills**
- eating out
- inviting someone to your home
- making suggestions

**Grammar**
- the partitive article : **du, de l', de la, des, pas de**
- the verbs **boire, venir** and **manger**
- questions with **quel**
- **moi, toi, lui, elle**
- **il y a**
- on = **nous**

**Vocabulary**
- expressions of quantity
- meals

*Page 48*

**La pause de midi** = the midday/lunch break. As almost everyone in France downs tools at 12 noon, the lunch break is referred to as the midday break, whether or not lunch is eaten at exactly that time.

**Le salé** = savoury food. **Le sucré** = sweet food.

See notes on P.52 about the partitive article, **du, de l', de la** and **des**.

*Page 49*

**Le Bistrot** (which can also be spelt **bistro**) is a café serving a limited range of food.

As this is a seaside café, it is not surprising to find that **moules** (mussels) with **frites** (chips) are being offered as **le plat du jour** (the dish of the day).

**Le menu à 80 F**. Set menus like this 80 F one are usually a better bargain than choosing different dishes **à la carte**. Two options are given for each of the three courses.

**Crudités** are raw vegetables, often diced or grated, with vinaigrette sauce, made from oil and vinegar.

**Charcuterie** is cold meats.

The extra light, quick snack for 30 francs is cold meat and salad.

A waiter can be either **un serveur** or **un garçon (de café)**

**J'arrive** - I'm coming; **L'addition** = the bill.

**Un renseignement** = a piece of information.

*Page 50*

**Au Soleil de Provence**. Provence is a Mediterranean region in south-east France.

**Une enquête** is a survey. In this case customers are being asked to comment on the restaurant and make **suggestions** (propositions or suggestions). As very few

French people are vegetarians, a vegetarian dish is not offered at lunch time.

Note that **cher** can mean "dear" in the sense of "expensive".

**Viens** is the **tu** form and **venez** is the **vous** form of the verb **venir** = to come.

*Page 51*

1. This is another example of the French predilection for surveys and statistics. In spite of the average lifetime consumption of 21,000 baguettes, the consumption of bread is falling quite rapidly in France, as more and more people can afford to buy a greater variety of foods and also more expensive food, like meat. Hence the large consumption of cattle and pigs. The average consumption of 2,000 kilos of cheese is perhaps to be expected in a country which makes hundreds of different kinds of cheese.

2. **Une salle** is a room used for a special purpose, in this case, for eating in a restaurant.

**Une assiette** here means a "plate" but it can also mean a "dish", as in **une assiette de crudités** or **une assiette de charcuterie**. **Une cuillère** can also be spelt **cuiller**. As the French drink more coffee than tea, a small spoon or teaspoon is **une cuiller à café**. Apart from **une cuiller à soupe** for a soup spoon, there are no special words for a dessert spoon or a tablespoon, just **une cuiller** or **une grande cuiller**.

*Page 52*

When "some" refers to an unspecified quantity of something, the word used before a masculine, singular noun is **du** (**du pain**), **de la** is used before a feminine, singular noun, (**de la viande**), **de l'** before a singular noun beginning with a vowel (**de l'eau**) and **des** before a plural noun, (**des jus de fruits**).

After the negative **de** is used, (**Je ne mange pas de pain, je ne bois pas d'eau**).

The interrogative **quel** agrees with the noun to which it refers. **Quel plat?** but **quelle viande?** etc.

The strong pronouns are used for emphasis, as in **Moi, je travaille, lui, il va au cinéma**, and also after prepositions, as in **chez moi, avec lui.**

Verbs whose infinitive ends in **-ger**, like **manger** and **voyager** need an **e** after the **g** in **nous mangeons, nous voyageons** in order to keep the **g** soft.

**On** is used a great deal in French as a substitute for "We", as in **Nous, on va au cinéma**.

### DIALOGUE A

**La cinq** here refers to "table, number 5".

French people eat more veal (**veau**) than British people. Spinach (**les épinards**) is also a popular dish.

**Le cassoulet** is a speciality of south-west France and is a stew of duck, pork or mutton with haricot beans.

**J'aimerais** and **je voudrais** both mean "I would like".

Notice the negative form **pas de** as in **pas de frites** = no chips and **pas d'alcool** = no alcohol.

**Un demi** is a glass of beer (a half-pint).

### DIALOGUE B

**La ligne** = figure;   **mince comme un fil** = thin as a rake (un fil is a thread or wire);   **Qu'est-ce qu'il y a?** = What is the matter?; **les adolescents** = teenagers; **personne** = nobody.

Note that **hors d'oeuvre** is invariable.  It is the same in the plural as in the singular.  This is the case with some other compound nouns like **porte-monnaie** = a purse.

# UNIT 6 Sport et santé

**Skills**
- saying that you are ill
- going to see the doctor
- giving advice

**Grammar**
- verbs **faire** and **dire**
- perfect tense with **avoir**
- questions: **combien de**
- the pronoun **en**
- **il faut** + infinitive

**Vocabulary**
- the human body
- sport
- quantity

*Page 56*

**J'ai mal à...** In French, to say that there is something wrong with you, all you need to say is **J'ai mal à** and then name the part of the body that is giving you trouble. So, **j'ai mal à la tête** = I have a headache, my head hurts, **j'ai mal à la gorge** = I have a sore throat, BUT remember that **J'ai mal au coeur** = I feel sick.

**The Perfect tense (passé composé)**

For the first time in this course you are describing a completed action in the past, saying what you have done or did. So **j'ai mangé un gâteau** = I ate, have eaten or did eat a cake.

*Page 57*

**Asseyez-vous** = Sit down; **je ne me sens pas bien** = I don't feel well;

**la grippe** = flu; **un comprimé** = a tablet.

*Page 58*

**Il faut** = It is necessary, you should, is used very often in French, as in **Il faut faire du sport** = You should/must take part in sport. This kind of encouragement may be needed by some French people, who give up sport as soon as they leave school and either ignore it completely or are content to watch other people doing it, probably on television. There is, however, a growing awareness of the need to keep fit, fostered by health and sports clubs of all kinds, and by books, newspapers and magazines which educate people on diet and healthy eating.

Notice that you can (**vous pouvez**) either **faire** or **pratiquer du sport**.

*Page 59*

It is well worth learning by heart all the parts of the body given on this page and noting any others that you may come across, such as **les dents** (f) = teeth or **le genou** = knee.

*Page 60*

More about the Perfect tense

Until the beginning of this unit all the verbs in **Café Crème** were in the present tense, describing an action that is taking place now or that usually takes place, so

**Je fais** = I do or I am doing. To describe an action that has already been completed in the past, you need to form the perfect tense by using part of the present tense of the verb **avoir**, followed by the past participle. For **–er** verbs the past participle ends in **-é** (**mangé, travaillé,** etc.) but as you can see on this page, a number of verbs have an irregular past participle (**eu, été, dit, fait** etc.) just as they do in English.

Notice that to form the negative of the perfect tense you must place the **ne** or **n'** before the appropriate part of **avoir** and the **pas** after it, and before the past participle, e.g. **Je n'ai pas mangé**.

*Page 61*

The pronoun **en** has various meanings, depending on the context. It can mean "some", "any" or "of it" or "of them". Look carefully at the examples given on this page to find the different meanings of **en** in English.

*Page 62*

**DIALOGUE A**

**Un moniteur** is an instructor teaching something where physical skill and coordination are needed, as in gymnastics, aerobics, skiing or driving a vehicle.

**Un professeur** teaches in a secondary school or university; **un instituteur** teaches in a primary school.

**Baissez** = lower; **étirez** = stretch; **rentrez** = pull in; **souriez** = smile.

**un cours** = a class or lesson.

The 70 year old lady who enjoys doing judo is proof that the French are taking fitness seriously and could be one of the reasons why life expectancy for French women is one of the highest in Europe.

**DIALOGUE B**

**Bouger** = to move; **être en pleine forme** = to be fully fit.

**Chapeau!** = congratulations! (I take off my hat to you)

*Pages 64 and 65*

The exercises on these two pages give you another opportunity to practise the work covered so far.

# UNIT 7 De toutes les couleurs

**Skills**
- giving advice
- giving your opinion
- buying
- finding your way about inside a large building

**Grammar**
- the demonstratives **ce, cet, cette** and **ces**
- measures of quantity; **beaucoup, très, assez,** and **trop**
- **je pense que**
- verbs **acheter, payer, finir** and **choisir**
- the ordinal numbers

**Vocabulary**
- colours
- clothes
- positions in space

*Page 66*

**Le marron** is used for the colour brown when describing clothes and shoes. As **le marron** is a noun meaning a chestnut the adjective of colour, marron, is invariable and does not add **-e** for the feminine or **-s** for the plural. **La châtaigne** is a sweet chestnut, from which comes the adjective of colour **châtain** meaning light brown, used to describe hair. **Le brun** also means brown and is used to describe dark brown hair, eyes or skin. **Être brun(e)** is to have dark hair.

**Roux** is used to describe red or auburn hair. Although there are some French people with auburn hair and quite a number with fair or blond hair, there are far more with dark-coloured hair.

**Essayer** = to try on and **un essai** is a trying on.

**Une glace** = a mirror

*Page 67 and 68*

In a large store **le rayon** is a department selling one type of goods. **Le bricolage** is DIY. Note too **bricoler** = to do odd jobs and **un bricoleur** = a person who does odd jobs.

**ameublement** (m) is furniture; **électro-ménager** is household electrical goods; **un jouet** = a toy; **la maroquinerie** = leather goods; **accueil** (m) = reception and **une librairie** is a bookshop. Remember that a library is **une bibliothèque**.

The different levels of a building are: **le sous-sol** = the basement, **le rez-de-chaussée** = the ground floor (sometimes given as just RC in lifts), **le premier étage** = the first floor, **le deuxième étage** = the second floor, **le dernier étage** = the top floor. Sometimes the word **le niveau** = the level is used instead of **étage**. Sometimes the word **étage** is omitted: **être au premier** = to be on the first floor.

Always look out for French words which look like English words but which have a different meaning. Apart from **la librairie** there are two of these on Page 68: **une veste** which is not "a vest" but "a jacket" and **large** which is not "large" but "wide".

Notice the way the customer gives her size: **Je fais du 40** and notice too the special meaning of **aller** in expressions like **le jaune vous va bien** = the yellow one suits you. Adjectives of colour are often used as pronouns, so **le jaune** is the yellow one, **ce rouge** is this red one.

*Page 69*

Payment can be made by cheque (**par chèque**), by cash (**en espèces**), or by a bank card (**carte bancaire**). A credit card is **une carte de crédit**.

**Sur** = on; **dessus** = on, over, above; **sous** = under; **dessous** = under, beneath.

*Page 70*

As **ce, cet, cette** and **ces** can mean either this or that and these or those, you can make the meaning clear by adding **-ci** for this, as in **cet homme-ci** = this man and **-là** for that, as in **cet homme-là** = that man.

*Page 71*

Note that **assez** = enough but when it is used before an adjective it means "quite" or "rather".

Be very careful how you use **beaucoup** and **très**. **Beaucoup** is used with a verb, as in **J'aime beaucoup la veste** = I like the jacket very much/a lot, but **très** is used with an adjective, as in **La veste est très jolie** = the jacket is very pretty. Although we can say very much in English, **très** and **beaucoup** canot be used together in French.

**Second(e)** which is pronounced as though the **c** were a **g** is used to describe the second of two, whereas **deuxième** describes the second of more than two. In some cases this distinction has become blurred, so that you can travel **en seconde** or **en deuxième classe**. There used to be three classes on French trains but now there are only two.

The personal pronouns **me, te, vous** and **lui** are all indirect object pronouns, that is, they suffer indirectly the action of the verb. **Cette couleur me va bien** - literally "This colour goes well with me", i.e. suits me.

*Page 72*

## DIALOGUE A

**Mode** is one of several words in French which has two genders; **Le mode** = the way (**le mode de vie** = the way of life) but **la mode** = fashion (**une boutique de mode** = a fashion shop, **un créateur de mode** = a fashion designer).

English has adopted the word boutique to mean a fashion shop, whereas French uses the word to mean either a fashion shop or any kind of small shop.

Although you can say **C'est combien?** for "How much is it?", you can also include **à** and say .... **ce pantalon, il est à combien?** Then the answer would probably be **il est à ....**

**J'ai passé un bon moment. Un moment** does not mean literally "a moment" but just a short period of time.

## DIALOGUE B

**J'en ai par-dessus la tête!** is one of several expressions meaning "I'm fed up, I've had enough". Others are **J'en ai assez! j'en ai marre! j'en ai ras-le-bol!**

**Allez** = Come on then; **les gens** = people (in general). When a specific number of people are referred to, the word used must be **personnes**, as in **Il y a 6 personnes dans la boutique** = There are 6 people in the shop.

**La robe est trop serrée** = the dress is too tight. **Serré** has various meanings, all to do with being squeezed together; **Je vous serre la main** = I shake your hand.

*Page 73*

**Un collant** = a pair of tights. **Coller** means to stick and **la colle** is glue. **Décoller** is to take off (an aeroplane).

# UNIT 8 Un aller retour

**Skills**
- understanding station announcements
- travelling by train
- going on holiday
- saying what you like

**Grammar**
- the perfect tense with **être**
- the verbs **partir, descendre, vouloir, pouvoir, devoir**
- use of **alors**
- position and agreement of adjectives

**Vocabulary**
- holiday activities
- expressions of time:
  **souvent, rarement, tous les jours, la semaine/l'année dernière, en retard, en avance, à l'heure**

*Page 74*

The railway station is **la gare** (**S.N.C.F.**), the coach station is **la gare routière** and the underground station is **la station (de métro)**.

To get into a vehicle is **monter (dans)** and to get out is **descendre (de)**. French trains are still high above the platform and have to be climbed into, so the reason for these verbs is apparent.

**La correspondance** is nothing to do with writing letters here but means the connecting train; **le quai** is the platform and **la voie** is the track.

*Page 75*

Notice that the noun **le départ** = departure begins with de in both English and French, but the French verb **partir** = to depart, leave, does NOT begin with **de**.

**Les renseignements** usually just means information. Here it is short for the information desk or office, **le bureau de renseignements. Au guichet** = at the ticket office. **Le guichet** is also a ticket office at the cinema, theatre etc.

Notice the use of the 24 hour clock for the timetables.

*Page 76*

Careful! **rester** = to remain and NOT to rest.

**En train** = by train. It is possible to say **par le train** and **par le bateau** but when talking about a means of transport it is usual to say **en**. Other examples are **en voiture, en taxi, en avion, en vélo, en car,** and **en camion**. Yet on foot is **à pied** and on horse-back is **à cheval**.

**La revue** (the magazine); **Tout m'intéresse** recalls the monthly magazine **Ça M'intéresse** which contains articles about all kinds of very interesting things.

*Page 77*

**Les loisirs** = leisure time; **une exposition** = an exhibition; **une randonnée** = a hike.

**Dernier**. Note that the expressions of time using **dernier** all refer to the one that has just gone by, e.g. **la semaine dernière** or **le week-end dernier**. When the last one is the last in a series, the position of **dernier** changes, e.g. **la dernière semaine des vacances** = the last week of the holidays.

**En avance** and **en retard** are early and late in the sense of before and after a pre-arranged time, whereas **tôt** and **tard** are early and late in the day, in life etc. **À l'heure** = on time.

*Page 78*

**LE PASSÉ COMPOSÉ AVEC ÊTRE** - THE PERFECT TENSE WITH *TO BE*

The Perfect tense is not always formed from the present tense of **avoir** + the past participle. In the case of certain verbs of movement, it is formed from the present tense of **être** + the past participle. There are 13 of these verbs as well as their compounds, (other verbs formed from them): **aller, venir, arriver, partir, entrer, sortir, rester, retourner, monter, descendre, tomber, naître** and **mourir**.

Do not forget that the past participle of these verbs must agree with the subject, so that an **e** is added for a feminine subject and an **s** for a plural subject.

*Page 79*

Note that the adjectives that are placed before rather than after the noun are all adjectives that are used very often. In some cases the adjective has become part of the noun, e.g. **une jeune fille** = a girl.

*Page 80*

**DIALOGUE A**

**Les vacances organisées** are package holidays.

**Le troisième âge** = the years of retirement of senior citizens.

Holiday clubs (**les clubs de vacances**) are popular in France, especially those like **Le Club Méditerranée**, where holidaymakers can join in many organised activities.

**DIALOGUE B**

**Bien joué!** = well played! As in English the past participle is used alone, with the **Vous avez** understood.

**Un palace** is a luxury hotel. A palace is **un palais**.

**La tournée** is a round of drinks. It can also mean a doctor's round or a postman's round.

*Page 81*

The Travel Agency is called ARC-EN-CIEL. **Un arc-en-ciel** is a rainbow.

## COULEURS COLOURS

Certain colours are found in all French towns, for example, the blue and white street plaques, but there are differences between different areas, especially the north and the south. In the sunny south, white and bright colours dominate, whereas in the north there are greys and darker hues, as in the granite roofs of Brittany and the half-timbers of Normandy.

There are also differences in the shape of buildings, in the number of storeys. Anyone who has been to Honfleur can hardly have failed to notice the lovely old many-storied buildings around the harbour.

**l'écrit** is what is written. In the street this is shop signs and names, advertisements, hoardings etc.

*Photos*

Nice has a population of about 350,000 and is an important tourist centre on the Riviera, with some splendid museums of modern art.

**Le boulevard Haussmann** with its high bourgeois buildings was named after the Prefect of the Seine, responsible for the building of the wide boulevards which transformed Paris in the nineteenth century.

**Une mansarde** is an attic room with a sloping roof, named after the seventeenth century architect, Mansard, who first designed this kind of room.

**Une colonne Morris** is one of the colourful, cylindrical kiosks used in Paris to advertise cinemas, theatres and other entertainments.

Lille has a population of one million and is a city of trade and industry, especially textiles. It was one of the capitals of the Dukes of Burgundy before it became part of France in 1667.

**Le Printemps** is a large department store in the boulevard Haussmann, built at the end of the nineteenth century.

*Page 83*

The French change the names of their streets quite often, as they are fond of commemorating the names of famous people, especially generals and other famous soldiers. Hence the **Place de l'Etoile** in the centre of Paris was renamed the **Place Charles de Gaulle**. The street names in Alsace reflect the changing fortunes of the region. When the Germans occupied Alsace in 1940, early in the second world war, they changed the French street names and shop names into German ones. At the end of the war, the French changed the German names back into French ones.

*Page 84*

**Une brasserie** is a brewery and so gave its name to the first establishments which sold beer and other drinks. Brasseries now also offer a limited range of meals as well as selling tobacco and stamps.

# PARTIE 3 Dis pourquoi...

*In Part 3 you will learn how to*
- *understand and explain about difficulties in obtaining employment*
- *prepare a CV in order to apply for a job*
- *understand and explain about family situations and relationships*
- *give your daily timetable*
- *understand and analyse some social changes*
- *show appreciation*
- *ask for and give or refuse advice*
- *understand and write about traffic problems*
- *apologise in a formal situation*

## The world of work

France, like the United Kingdom, has suffered greatly from **la crise** - the recession - of the nineteen nineties.

French companies, bound by the Social Chapter of the Treaty of Maastricht, have not been able to restructure industry as quickly as some British firms.

Whilst President Chirac's government is proceeding slowly with its privatisation policy, much of French industry still relies on government subsidy and management is struggling to contend with militant unions, calling out staff to strike if their jobs, salaries or working conditions are threatened.

In the summer of 1997 the unemployment figures in France were 12.6% compared to 5.7% in the United Kingdom.

The young in France are particularly vulnerable to **le chômage** - unemployment - with one in four young people under the age of 25 unable to find work, in spite of the government's attempts to give incentives to firms who create jobs for them.

However, although France still has a large deficit in its gross national product, French industry is showing signs of coming out of the recession. Much of the labour force is skilled and highly qualified, with many firms at the forefront of **la technologie de pointe** (high tech.). There are signs that French workers are adapting to change and becoming more used to the prospect of having to change direction several times during their career. Some young people are showing great initiative in finding a market niche in which to use their talents.

## Training

In a changing world education and training (**la formation**) are becoming more and more important.

Hence the increasing number of students passing the school leaving examination (**le baccalauréat**), and who then do further training in the form of work experience or a vocational course (**un stage**).

We are told on Page 94 that 58% of the French believe that the family is more important than love, in spite of the fact that fewer people are marrying and more people are divorcing. We learn, too, that relationships within families are changing, with parents being less autocratic and attempting to understand their children better. Fathers are playing a greater part in the upbringing of their children, with a few even taking a year or more off work in order to look after their young children, whilst the mother goes out to work. Where parents divorce, each continues to take responsibility for the children, who often share their time between their mother and father. When grandparents live near, they, too, may play their part in the family life.

## Social Life

With "culture" highly considered in a country whose Minister of Culture spends more than a billion pounds a year, it is not surprising if town councillors have the power to give grants to help the young unemployed to take part in amateur theatre.

Although café life may be suffering from people's reluctance to leave their television set in order to go out and socialise in a café or bar, it is encouraging that some café proprietors are succeeding in their efforts to encourage customers to frequent their establishments.

The enjoyment of café life has long been a great attraction of France for foreigners.

## Transport

France, which has 18% of the cars currently being driven

**27**

in Europe, has the same environmental problems as Britain. Although France is twice the size of Britain, a fifth of the French population is crowded into the Paris region, so that the number of cars entering the capital every working day exceeds the number of parking places available.

It is no wonder that the government endeavours to encourage public transport. Unfortunately, recent strikes by public transport workers have made life very difficult for those who work in Paris. Many have resorted to buying bicycles in their desperate attempt to get to and from work. Although France has a large network of motorways, trunk roads and country roads, some of these are overcrowded at rush hours and at peak holiday times. **Le Périphérique**, the ring road around Paris, is sometimes so crowded that, like the M25 in England, traffic is brought to a halt for long periods.

# UNIT 9 **Au travail!**

**Skills**
- understanding the reason for an
  event in a written text
- asking and giving information
  about a job advertisement

**Grammar**
- questions:  **pourquoi**
- the comparative
- **à cause de, parce que**
- prepositions of time
- prepositions before names of
  countries

**Vocabulary**
- work experience
- following a career

*Page 86*

**Dans les années 90** = in the nineties. Hence **dans les
années 70** = the seventies etc.

**Les salariés** = people who receive **un salaire** (a salary).

**Un chômeur** is a person who is **au chômage**
(unemployed).

**Un responsable** is the person in charge, manager.

**Un CV (curriculum vitae)** is one of many Latin phrases
used in modern French. Other popular ones are **grosso
modo** = more or less, roughly, and **à priori** = in
principle, (on the basis of what has already happened).

**Circuler** = to go around; **Un VTT (vélo tout terrain)** =
mountain bike.

Bicycles and mopeds have long been a popular form of
transport in France, especially in country districts.
Parisians have recently taken to the bicycle as a last
resort during the public transport strikes.

**Une demande d'emploi** = a job application; **créer** = to
found; **un coursier** = a messenger, errand boy; **un
concurrent** = a competitor.

*Page 87*

**Une offre d'emploi** = a job offer. These often appear in
the section of newspapers called **Les Petites
Annonces** (small ads).

The example on this page is typical of this kind of
advertisement in its layout and in its use of words.
**Recherche** or **cherche** are the verbs usually used for
"looking for". As newspaper or magazine space is
expensive, it is important to use as few words as
possible. Hence the sentence beginning **Contrat....** has
no article and no verb. Initial letters (**sigles**) are much in
evidence, as in **P.M.E.** for a **Petite ou Moyenne
Entreprise** (small or medium sized firm).

*Page 88*

**L'ANPE (Agence nationale pour l'emploi)** is another
**sigle**. It is the equivalent of our Job Centre. The job
applicant is asked if he speaks any foreign languages as
he would be required to visit customers abroad. It is

becoming more and more important for French people
to speak other languages, as an increasing number of
businesses cooperate or merge with companies abroad.
**Un treizième mois** is an extra month's salary paid at
the end of the year.

*Page 89*

**La formation** is training as opposed to studies. **Un
stage** can be work experience for a student or it can be
a training course for a member of staff or a period of
time spent in a different department or job.

**Un cadre** is any kind of manager or executive, whether
it be a director of a company or someone in middle or
junior management. The degrees of seniority can be
given by **un cadre supérieur/moyen/ inférieur**= a
senior/middle/junior manager.

A CV usually contains a reference to the owner's **état
civil,** stating whether s/he is married **marié(e)** or single
(**célibataire**). **Célibataire** also has the meaning of
"celibate".

(**être**) **à la recherche** = (to be) looking for.

*Page 90*

Most countries are feminine in French. "In" or "to" before
a feminine country is **en, (en France)** but before a
masculine country it is **au, (au Japon)** and before a
plural country it is **aux (aux Pays-Bas)**. "From" is **de** or
**d'** before a feminine country (**de France, d'Italie**), **du**
before a masculine country (**du Canada**) and **des**
before a plural country (**des États-Unis**).

**Parce que** (because) needs a verb after it but **à cause
de** (because of) needs a subordinate clause, e.g. <u>**À
cause du** chômage</u> and <u>**Parce qu'**il n'y a pas assez
de travail</u>.

*Page 91*

"Than" or "as" in a comparison is **que**, as in **Alain est
plus grand que Philippe** = Alain is taller than Philippe
or **Alain est aussi grand que David** = Alain is as tall as
David.

Look carefully at the examples given of the use of the
conjunctions **mais, parce que, alors, donc** and **pour.**

*Page 92*

## DIALOGUE A

The influence of English or American is evident in the world of jazz and popular music, so, instead of going to the **le club de jazz**, Patrick is going to **le jazz club.**

Patrick, like most young people in France, uses abbreviations for long words, **le saxo** for **le saxophone.**

Joseph, his father, uses the affectionate term **fiston** or "sonny" to his son.

In this context the verb **répéter** means "to rehearse" - **On répète** pour le concert.

**Bonne journée!** = Have a good day! This kind of well-wishing is very common in France. Similar expressions are: **Bon voyage!** = Have a good journey!, **Bon appétit!** = Enjoy your meal!, **Bonne chance**! = Good luck! and **Bonnes vacances!** = Have a good holiday!

Joseph says that music is **le sel de la vie** (the spice of life). This is a metaphor that is similar and yet different from the English one. Some proverbs are very alike, like

**Pierre qui roule n'amasse pas mousse** = A rolling stone gathers no moss, but others are different, like **Tomber de Charybde en Scylla** = to jump from the frying pan into the fire.

## DIALOGUE B

Antoine uses another abbreviation, **sympa** for **sympathique** (friendly, nice).

**Pourquoi ça n'a pas marché?** = Why didn't that work? **Ben** or **Bon ben** are just filling in words at the beginning of a sentence, like "Well then" in English. **Hé!** can also mean "Well" but here it means "Hey"!

**Un type** is "a fellow" or "bloke".

*Page 93*

4. The musical instruments are **un alto** = an alto saxophone; **un cor** = a horn; **un orgue** = an organ. **L'accordéon** = the accordion is, of course, especially popular in France.

5. Listen carefully to the way the voice rises when expressing surprise.

# UNIT 10 En famille

**Skills**
- understand the information given in a written text
- giving explanations to another person and understanding theirs
- giving your daily timetable

**Grammar**
- direct object pronouns: **le, la, l', les**
- comparisons
- the pronoun **en** in comparison
- verbs + infinitive with **à, de** or without a preposition

**Vocabulary**
- **jouer à / faire de**
- opposites of adjectives and verbs

*Page 94*

Annie, a young divorcee, with a six year old daughter, chooses to work from home so that she can spend as much time as possible with her little girl.

**Une compagnie d'assurances** = an insurance company.

**En fin de semaine** = at the end of the week. There are several other similar expressions of time, such as **en fin de matinée** = at the end of the morning, **and en fin d'après-midi** = at the end of the afternoon.

*Page 95*

**L'emploi du temps** = timetable; **le réveil** = alarm clock; **sonner** = to ring; **la sonnerie** = ringing; **faire sa toilette** = to have a wash. The verb **faire** is used for many domestic activities, e.g. **faire le ménage** (housework), **la lessive** (washing), **la vaisselle** = the washing up, **les lits** (the beds), **la cuisine** (cooking) and **le repassage** (ironing).

Annie starts work at 9.15 in the morning as she takes Sandra to school first, but the working day starts earlier for many French people. Most break for lunch at midday, but often this is just a short break, instead of the traditional long one, so that the working day will end sooner. This is called **la journée continue**.

*Page 96*

Note the theatrical vocabulary on this page: **le metteur en scène** = producer; **la scène** = stage; **monter une pièce** = to put on a play; **la représentation** = performance.

The idea of encouraging the unemployed to talk freely about their problems on the stage is an interesting one and certainly represents an attempt to do something partly to alleviate the problems caused by unemployment.

**revivre** = to relive or live again. The prefix **re** or **r can be placed at** the beginning of many verbs to give the idea of doing something again. Examples of this are **partir** and **repartir, entrer** and **rentrer, monter** and **remonter, faire** and **refaire.**

**Qu'est-ce que vous pensez de votre travail?** = What do you think about your work? **Penser** is followed by **de** when it has the meaning of forming an opinion about something. When **penser** means to think in the sense of a thought coming into someone's head, it is followed by **à**, e.g. **Je pense à mes vacances** = I am thinking of my holidays.

*Page 97*

**Jouer** is followed by **à, à l', au** or **aux** when it means to play a game, whether it be cards or sport, e.g. **jouer au football, jouer aux cartes,** and by **de, du, de l'** or **des** when it means to play a musical instrument, e.g. **jouer de l'orgue** or **jouer du piano. Jouer** also has the meaning of "to act" or "to play a part".

**Faire** can be used both for games and for musical instruments, e.g. **faire du tennis** and **faire de la trompette.**

*Page 98*

**The subject pronouns: je, tu, il, elle, on, nous, vous, ils,** and **elles** are the pronouns that replace the subject of the verb, e.g. **L'acteur** joue dans la pièce = **Il** joue dans la pièce.

**The direct object pronouns, me/m', te/t', le/l', la/l', nous, vous,** and **les**, are the pronouns that replace the direct object of the verb, e.g. J'aime **la musique** = Je l'aime.

Look carefully at other examples on this page, noting especially that the direct object pronoun is placed <u>before</u> the verb and not <u>after</u> it, as in English, e.g. **Vous prenez cette robe? - Oui, je la prends.**

In the Perfect tense, the direct object pronoun is placed before the auxiliary verb (avoir or être), e.g. **Vous avez fini votre travail? - Oui, je l'ai fini.**

In the present tense the negative **ne** is placed **before** the object pronoun and **pas** is placed **after** the verb or **after** the auxiliary verb in the perfect tense but **before** the past participle, e.g. - Vous prenez cette robe? - Non, je **ne la** prends pas. Vous avez fini votre travail? Non, je **ne l'ai pas fini.**

When the verb is conjugated with **avoir** in the perfect tense, the past participle agrees with the preceding direct object, e.g. **Où est-ce que tu as acheté cette veste? - Je l'ai acheté<u>e</u> dans une petite boutique** and - **Vous avez fini vos exercices? - Non, je ne <u>les</u> ai pas fin<u>is</u>.**

*Page 99*

Comparisons with expressions of quantity;

**plus de...que** = more than, e.g. **Michel a <u>plus de</u> travail <u>que</u> Xavier**;

**moins de...que** = less than, e.g. **Xavier a <u>moins de</u> travail <u>que</u> Michel**;

**autant de...que** = as much as, e.g. **Michel a <u>autant de</u> travail <u>que</u> Marc**.

These can all be used with the pronoun **en**, e.g. **Les ouvriers ont du travail mais Michel <u>en</u> a plus que Xavier.**

Many verbs can be directly followed by an infinitive, like **vouloir, pouvoir, détester, aimer, devoir, falloir,** and **adorer**, e.g. **Je veux partir en vacances.** Some verbs are followed by the preposition **à**, like **continuer à**, e.g. **Je continue à faire du théâtre.** Some verbs are followed by the preposition **de**, like **choisir de, finir de,** and **arrêter de**, e.g. **J'arrête de jouer.**

*Page 100*

**DIALOGUE A**

**Exposer** = to set out, explain.

**Un conseiller municipal** = a town councillor. Each of the 36,000 **communes** or areas of administrative government in France, has a town council, elected at the **élections municipales. Le maire** (the mayor) is elected from the town councillors and is an important member of the community. It is s(he) (or his/her assistant mayors or councillors) who marries couples and who makes decisions about how to spend the local budget.

In this case the town councillor agrees with Nathalie's idea about using children from a housing estate to act in a play but he quickly departs before she has time to ask for financial help.

**La cité** = housing estate; **traîner** = to hang around. **Être en train de** + infinitive is a good way of expressing in French what you are in the act of doing, what you are doing now. Nathalie says **Je suis en train de terminer une école de théâtre** = I am finishing off drama school.

**DIALOGUE B**

**Rentrer** (with or without **à la maison**) means to go back home as well as to re-enter.

**Avoir raison** = to be right; Another verb which uses **avoir** whereas English says "to be right".

**Il faut** = You need (literally = It is necessary). This use of the impersonal verb **falloir** is very common in French.

It is now Joseph's turn to receive a mysterious message, a phone call from a man called Pierre who appears to know him. Could this be the same person as the mysterious P. who wrote to Jacques Mistral?

*Page 101*

3. Remember that **mille** is invariable. It remains the same in the singular and plural, **mille =** one thousand and **onze mille** = eleven thousand.

4. Imitate the rise and fall of the voice in exclamations.

6. **Un parking** = a car park. This is an English word whose meaning has been changed in French. Similarly **un caravanning** = a caravan site. Parking = **le stationnement**.

7. **par écrit** = in writing.

*Pages 102 and 103*

**BILAN**

Note that a family is referred to as **Les Léger** or **Les Roy** whereas English would add the plural **s,** The Léger<u>s</u> or The Roy<u>s</u>.

# UNIT 11 Autour d'un verre

**Skills**
- understanding and analysing a
  social event in a written text
- understanding/expressing purpose
- expressing appreciation
- asking/giving/refusing advice

**Grammar**
- indirect object pronouns: **lui, leur**
- the verbs **plaire, écrire, vivre** and
  **envoyer**
- the immediate future: **aller** +
  infinitive
- the superlative of adjectives

**Vocabulary**
- **quelqu'un, quelque chose**
  **ne...personne / ne...rien**
- words for expressing opinion

---

*Page 104*

When you have digested all the facts and figures given in
this article about modern France, consider if the same
sort of changes are taking place in your own country.

**Il y a** here means "ago" and not "There is" or "there are".
**Un lieu de rencontres** = a meeting place; **la
disparition** = disappearance. **Actuel** is one of the
French words that looks like an English word, but which
does not have the same meaning. So **actuel** does NOT
mean "actual" - it means "current". **À l'heure actuelle** =
now, at the moment.

*Page 105*

**Un lycéen** is a student at **un lycée** = the secondary
school at which students prepare for **le baccalauréat.**

Most **lycées** serve quite a large area and so, in a
populated area, will have quite a large number of
students. The lycée Voltaire has 1,300 students.

**La sortie** = exit, so **à la sortie de** = on leaving. **La
cantine** may not please all the students all the time, but
the food offered in French schools and other institutions
is often very good, the menus balanced and carefully
worked out. The sandwiches sold in the **Petit bistrot**
are probably French type sandwiches, made from
baguettes. English type sandwiches are quite popular in
France since the arrival of shops like Marks and Spencer.

Myriam, the proprietor's daughter, is also the waitress,
and is able to discuss all kinds of subjects with her
student friends. Like many a publican or bartender in
England, the proprietor (**le patron**) is on good terms with
his customers and enjoys their company. As Françoise
says, **Le patron nous aime bien** = The boss likes us.

**Un concours** = a competition. The competition here is
for the "youngest" café in the district, otherwise, the café
which best suits young people. Even the opening hours
of **Le Petit bistrot**, from 8am until 7pm, are to suit
young people, who may like to breakfast in the café
before school and meet there before returning home for
dinner in the evening.

As the **patron** even organises a party just before the
summer holidays for his customers, where the non-
alcoholic drinks are free, it is no surprise that **Le Petit
bistrot** won the competition. Although France is one of
the major wine drinking countries in the world, many
young people enjoy non-alcoholic drinks, like coca cola,
lemonade, orangina and milk.

*Page 106*

**Tomber amoureux** = to fall in love; **Elle te plaît?** = Do
you like her? **rigoler** = to laugh, have a giggle; **un petit
mot** = a note, short letter; **le ciné** = an abbreviation of
**le cinéma. Tu parles!** = You must be joking!

*Page 107*

**Tout** = all, everything; **quelque chose** = something,
anything and **quelqu'un** = someone are all positive,
whereas **ne...rien**, and **ne... personne** are negative.
Notice the position of the **ne** and the **rien** in **Je ne
prends rien** = I won't have anything and in **rien n'est
tombé** = nothing fell. **Personne** can also begin the
sentence, as in **Personne n'a appelé** or it can be
placed after the verb, as in **Non, je ne cherche
personne** and **Non, il n'y a personne**.

Answer the **enquête** or questionnaire to find out how
your restaurant habits compare with those of your fellow
students.

*Page 108*

The indirect object pronouns, **me, m', te, t', lui, nous,
vous** and **leur** usually replace a noun preceded by the
preposition **à.** In English the word "to" or "for" is
sometimes implied rather than expressed, so that we say
"I write <u>him</u> a letter" instead of "I write a letter <u>to</u> him" or
"I buy <u>her</u> a present" instead of "I buy a present <u>for</u> her".
Notice that **lui** and **leur** are the only indirect object
pronouns which have a different form from the
corresponding direct oject pronouns. Like the direct
object pronouns, the indirect object pronouns usually
precede the verb, e.g. **Je <u>lui</u> parle** or **Je <u>lui</u> ai parlé**.
The strong or emphatic pronouns **moi, toi, lui, elle,
nous, vous, eux** and **elles** are used after a preposition
e.g. **Il habite chez <u>moi</u>** and **Annie parle de <u>toi</u>** and
they are also used in a comparison, e.g. **Nous avons
autant de problèmes qu'<u>eux</u>**.

*Page 109*

**The Immediate Future**

To say what you are going to do, use the appropriate form of the present tense of **aller** + the infinitive, e.g. **Je vais partir** = I am going to leave or **Il ne va pas partir** = he is not going to leave.

The superlative of adjectives is formed from the definite article followed by **plus** or **moins**, e.g. **Cette veste est la moins chère; les chaussettes sont les plus chères**.

The superlative of **bon** is **le/la/les meilleur(es)**

"In" after a superlative is often translated by **de**, e.g. **On trouve les meilleurs sandwiches d'Orléans au Petit bistrot** = You find the best sandwiches in Orleans at the Petit bistrot.

*Page 110*

**DIALOGUE A**

**Un de perdus...dix de retrouvés!** = There are more fish in the sea! **Fondre en larmes** = to burst into tears; **discuter** = to talk about; **renifler** = to sniff; **se moucher** = to blow one's nose; **faire la fête** = to have a party, celebrate; **le boulot** = work, job.

**DIALOGUE B**

**Allez!** = Come on!; **Qu'est-ce qu'il joue bien!** = How well he acts!; **le plus fort** = the best; **une bande dessinée** = cartoon (often called a **B.D.**)

Cartoons are very popular in France and considered as serious literature. Some of the best, like Astérix and Hergé's adventures of Tintin are well-known in England as well. An annual festival is held in Angoulême, where there is a splendid modern centre for this form of art. The French government has recently announced a whole series of measures designed to encourage and develop **la B.D**.

*Page 111*

6. This kind of personal advertisement often appears in a column called **Le courrier du coeur**. As in Britain, this is a popular and growing area of journalism.

Apart from writing an advertisement to describe yourself you might like to invent further advertisements about people you know or invent.

# UNIT 12 Embouteillages

**Skills**
- understanding and writing a text giving information
- apologising and justifying yourself in a formal situation

**Grammar**
- the Future tense
- the negative
- questions: preposition + **qui**
- the verb **savoir**

**Vocabulary**
- buildings in a town
- giving the sequence of events
- apologising

---

*Page 112*

**Savoir** is "to know a fact" or "to know how to do something". In the sentence **La France a toujours su innover dans les transports** the verb has the meaning of "knowing how".

**Le Concorde** is a supersonic jet passenger plane flying between America and Europe, which is still in service but has proved rather expensive in proportion to the small number of passengers that it can carry.

There has recently been a resurgence of interest, both in France and England, in trams as a cheap, non-polluting means of public transport. There are new trams in Brest in the west of France and Strasbourg in the east.

**Évoluer** = to develop, progress.

There are, of course, already cars powered by electricity and there are also computer systems which help drivers to find the best route to their destination, and which give information on any obstacles.

*Page 113*

Rennes is the capital of Brittany, with a population of about 450,000.

**Une place de parking** = a parking spot; **les transports en commun** = public transport.

Perhaps more provincial towns will follow the example of Rennes and build a silent, non-polluting underground system. La Rochelle, a town of about 160,000 inhabitants on the Atlantic coast, has done a great deal to encourage tourists by endeavouring to make movement about the town easier. Some years ago the local council introduced yellow bicycles which people could use to move about the town. The bicycles were free for the first few hours and then a small fee was charged. The problem was that the bicycles had to be returned by early evening and many simply disappeared. Perhaps it will not be so easy to steal the electric cars that La Rochelle is now offering its visitors.

*Page 114*

Most students will sympathise with the problems caused by traffic jams to the lady in this dialogue.

One way of apologising is **je suis désolé(e)**. Other ways are **je suis ennuyé(e)** or **je regrette**.

**Être de retour** is "to be back".

Although we now use the metric system we continue to talk about "a dozen" whereas the French say either **une douzaine** or **une dizaine** (about ten). You can add the suffix **-aine** to other numbers to indicate a vague number, e.g. **une vingtaine, une cinquantaine** or **une centaine**.

*Page 115*

It is very easy to obtain a street plan of the town you are visiting if you ask for one at the **Syndicat d'initiative** or **l'Office du tourisme**.

Notice the way that the date is given in French, **Aujourd'hui, nous sommes le 15 décembre.** You can also say **C'est aujourd'hui le 15 décembre.**

*Page 116*

**Le futur simple** or simple future tense does not exist in English. To say what will take place in the future we say "I will do, you will do" etc.

As you can see on this page, the future tense in French is formed from the infinitive of regular **-er** and **-ir** verbs plus the present tense of the verb **avoir**. Hence, **j'aimerai, tu aimeras, il aimera** etc. You will notice that there are quite a lot of irregular forms, but that these have the same endings as the regular forms.

Learn carefully the forms of the irregular verb **savoir**, noting especially its imperative forms.

*Page 117*

Study the chart of the negatives, particularly noting the position of **personne** in **Je n'ai parlé à personne. Qui?** is used when asking questions about people, to mean "Who?" or "Whom?". Notice how **qui** combines with the prepositions **à, de, avec** and **pour.**

*Page 118*

**DIALOGUE A**

**Rouler** = to drive along, to move (of a vehicle); **être pressé** = to be in a hurry.

**Dans** is always used for "in" when referring to future time, as in **Votre avion part dans combien de temps? Dans deux heures**.

Although the **ne** of the negative should always be included in written French, it is often omitted in the spoken language, e.g. **t'es pas un peu fou**. The **u** of **tu** should also always be used in written French.

**Qu'est-ce que vous voulez?** = What do you expect? **Voyager** = to travel in the general sense, but **se déplacer** is to move about or to travel for a particular purpose, as for business.

### DIALOGUE B

**Libre** = free, in the sense of "still for hire".

**Il y en a plein ma valise.** This is a colloquial way of saying "My case is full of it". **La monnaie** = change because **une pièce de monnaie** = a coin. The mysterious Pierre is speaking on Joseph's taxiphone again, this time to arrange a meeting for the next day at the Paris-Lyon Palace (a hotel).

*Page 119*

3. Do you know all the items of clothing in this list?

**Un tailleur** = a suit (for a female); **un gilet** = a waistcoat;

**un maillot de bain** = a swimming costume.

4. **Être en colère** = to be angry. Listen to and imitate the rise and fall of the voice when expressing anger.

**Laissez-moi tranquille** = leave me alone/in peace; **Vous ne pouvez pas regarder devant vous**? = Can't you look where you're going?

*Page 120*

### RYTHMES

Notice that every Sunday in the French calendar is underlined. Public holidays like **JOUR DE L'AN** (New Year's day) and **ARMISTICE** are written in capital letters and some religious festivals are in bold letters - **Mardi-Gras** (Shrove Tuesday) and **Carême** (Lent), as well as some special days, like **Jour du Souvenir**, a day to remember the Jews who were sent to German concentration camps in the second world war. The 27 April 1945 was the date that the camps at Dachau and Auschwitz were liberated.

Although school holidays do vary a little from region to region in the United Kingdom, there is no strict division into three geographical zones as there is in France. The idea of this is that it will prevent everyone from travelling at exactly the same time and so cut down on traffic jams and road accidents.

May is the month of the year during which the French enjoy more public holidays (**jours fériés**) than any other.

*Page 121*

### Photos

Just as there are the seven wonders of the world, the cinema is the seventh art (**le septième art**). Cannes, a seaside town on the Riviera, with a population of about 70,000, has, since 1946, held an annual film festival. Celebrities from all over the world come to take part and find out who has won the coveted first prize - **La Palme d'or**.

The **Roland-Garros** stadium, in the south of Paris, near the Bois de Boulogne, is the venue for the annual French national tennis championships, one of the four most important in the world - the other three being the All-England tennis championships at Wimbledon, and the American and Australian open championships.

**Le Tour de France** which began in 1903 is now the most important cycling race in the world and one of the world's most demanding sporting events. Held every July, it always ends with thousands of people cheering the winner arriving in Paris at the Champs-Elysées. The tour starts from a different place every year and now always has one stage abroad, either in Spain, Italy or even Britain. The competitors are followed by **la caravane publicitaire** - a colourful cavalcade of advertising vehicles - and thousands of French people spend their annual holiday cheering on the cyclists as they pass through the towns and villages of France.

**La journée du patrimoine** is the day when the French celebrate their national inheritance.

*Page 122*

**La Chandeleur** is Candlemas.

**La galette des Rois**, the special cake for Epiphany traditionally contains **une fève**, a bean. The person who receives the bean in his or her portion of the cake is crowned king or queen and can choose his/her consort.

**Les crêpes** used to be the food of the poor but are now the speciality of Brittany, where there are many **Crêperies**.

# PARTIE 4 **Alors raconte...**

*In Part 4 you will learn how to:*
- *tell stories about what has happened to you and to other people in the past, setting the scene, describing people and their character and recounting the sequence of events*
- *explain how you feel about things, expressing different emotions of pleasure, fear etc.*
- *find your way about*
- *find out and give measurements*
- *describe living accommodation*

## THE DREAM AND THE REALITY

In this final part of Café Crème we are made aware of the complexities of life in France today, of the life people imagine and the life they really live. In some cases we see how the reality of their present life measures up or does not measure up to youthful hopes and dreams. These people talk about their ambitions and what they have so far achieved. They talk about where they live and why they live there, the holidays they have had and those that they plan to have, and about what stirs their emotions.

The picture that finally emerges is a complex one and leaves many questions unanswered - not the least of these being the future of Pierre and Liliane in **Les Paroles en Liberté.** Will these two "get together" after so many years, or is it too late for them to do so?

## CAREERS

Many people change direction in their working life because they do not succeed in the career they initially chose. Fanny Ardant wanted to be an opera singer but became an actress. Martine was a ballerina at the Opéra but became the proprietor of a small café in Toulouse.

Others succeed in their chosen careers. Jacques seems to be doing well as an architect and Joseph is quite content to remain a singing taxi driver. Hélène is about to take up a new post as the boss of her former boyfriend.

Very many people from all over France come to work in the capital, as it is so much the centre of the country's economic and business life. Some enjoy living in or near Paris with its shops and restaurants, theatres and cinemas and art galleries, but others prefer to move away to the country. In the case of one young man the reason for this is just that his wife prefers to stay in the region in which she grew up and he, too, has now fallen in love with that region.

## HOLIDAYS

As children many French people are sent to a **Colonie de Vacances** or special children's holiday camp, where young leaders, usually students, look after the children and organise many outdoor and indoor activities. In the meantime parents can spend their own holidays as they please, perhaps visiting relatives, renting accommodation in the mountains, countryside or near the sea or even staying in a hotel.

Others will go to their **résidence secondaire** or second home. 13% of the French own one of these, more than the people of any other European nation. Very often the second home was once the family home in the country or belonged to the grandparents or parents who had perhaps joined the **exode rural**. This was the movement to towns in order to seek work in the new factories and businesses that sprang up after the industrial revolution, which came later in France than it did in England.

Those who do not possess a second home can enjoy the peace and natural life of the many regional and national parks.

## WORLD OF IMAGINATION AND EMOTION

The imaginative young man who believes that he has witnessed a horrible murder and Pierre, who imagines devious ways of bringing his University friends together, are just two of the French people in Café Crème who reveal the imaginative power of the nation. Throughout the course we have seen the love of the French for the arts, for music, the cinema, the theatre and literature.

The final **Civilisation** section, on Paris, illustrates the pride the French take in their rich, cultural heritage and their determination to preserve and embellish this heritage in the future.

# UNIT 13 Souvenirs d'enfance

**Skills**
- talking about oneself
- recounting events in the past and situating them in the past

**Grammar**
- the Imperfect tense
- the difference between the use of the Imperfect and the Perfect
- **il y a**
- time clauses with **quand**
- the verb **connaître**

**Vocabulary**
- words to express feelings

*Page 124*

See the notes for page 128 in the next column for the formation and use of the Imperfect.

The text **C'était en été** is full of short sentences including verbs, as the young man is looking back into the past and evoking a series of romantic memories.

The last paragraph, too, is made up of three short sentences, as the young man comes down to earth with a bump!

**Cher ami**. This term can be used affectionately but here it is tinged with irony.

The adjective **futur** is placed in the unemphatic position before the noun in order to give extra emphasis to the noun (**chef**) itself.

*Page 125*

Fanny Ardant was the companion to the famous filmmaker, François Truffaut, 1932-1984, who made gentle, largely autobiographical films like **Les quatre cents coups** and **Jules et Jim**. Fanny won an Oscar in 1997 for her part in Patrick Lecomte's film **Ridicule**.

**Don Juan** is an opera played at the Mozart festival in Aix-en-Provence.

**Gagner sa vie** = to earn one's living; **une répétition** = a rehearsal;

**fou** can be both an adjective meaning "mad" or a noun, as here, where **un fou** means a mad person.

*Page 126*

You will notice the mixture of tenses in this dialogue. The Present tense is used for what is happening at the time, the Perfect tense to talk about completed actions in the past and the Imperfect to describe a situation or say what used to happen.

**Quelle surprise!** = What a surprise!

**La fac.** is an abbreviation for **la faculté**.

**On habite à la campagne.** Here **on** = we.

When saying how far one place is from another, you must remember to include **à**, as in ....**la campagne, à**

**10 kilomètres du centre**.

If **savoir** = "to know a fact" or "to know how to", the verb **connaître** means "to know a person or a place". **Tu connais le Midi?** = Do you know the south of France? and **Tu me connais** = You know me.

**Un(e) libraire** = a bookseller and **un(e) bibliothécaire** = a librarian.

*Page 127*

French uses the infinitive where English uses a verbal noun, e.g. **Écouter de la musique.....** = Listening to music, **Parler de la guerre** = Talking of war, **Faire des cadeaux....** = giving presents.

*Page 128*

FORMATION OF THE IMPERFECT TENSE

The Imperfect tense is formed from the stem of the first person plural of the Present tense plus the endings **-ais, -ais, -ait, -ions, -iez** and **-aient**. The only exception to this rule is the verb **être** which adds the same endings to the stem (**le radical**) **ét**. giving **j'étais, tu étais, il était, nous étions, vous étiez, ils étaient.**

USE OF THE IMPERFECT AND THE PERFECT TENSES

Both tenses are used for describing past actions, but, whereas the Perfect tense describes a sequence of actions or a completed action which took place at a precise moment in the past, the Imperfect tense describes the situation, the background, the circumstances, habits and actions that were going on.

The English translation of the perfect tense **Le téléphone a sonné** could be "The telephone rang, has rung, did ring or has been ringing". The English translation of the imperfect tense **Le téléphone sonnait** could be "The telephone rang, was ringing, used to ring or would ring", as long as the implication is that the telephone went on ringing or rang on more than one occasion.

*Page 129*

Look carefully at the examples of sentences where **il y a** means "ago".

Learn the forms of **connaître** and note that there is a circumflex on the **î** of the infinitive and of the third person singular **connaît** but not on any of the other forms.

Study the use of tenses in subordinate clauses beginning with **quand**, especially noting the use of the future tense in the sentence **Quand vous viendrez à Paris, je vous inviterai à dîner.** Although English prefers the present tense in this kind of sentence, saying "When you come to Paris, I will invite you to dinner" the French is really more logical as the action of coming is not taking place now, in the present, but will take place in the future. This "hidden" future is also used in other similar time clauses beginning with **dès que** or **aussitôt que** = as soon as.

*Page 130*

### DIALOGUE A

When the verb **monter** is used to mean "to put/take/set up" rather than "to go up" it is conjugated with **avoir** instead of with **être**. Jacques says of the luggage **Quelqu'un les a montés** meaning "Someone has taken it up"and Liliane says **J'ai monté une entreprise** = I have set up a business. When **monter** is conjugated with **avoir** the past participle will, of course, agree with the preceding direct object and when it is conjugated with **être** the past participle will agree with the subject.

The verbs that are conjugated with **être** are all intransitive verbs, that is, they cannot have a direct object, but when they become transitive verbs they can have a direct object. Other verbs like this are **descendre, sortir** and **rentrer. J'ai descendu le livre de ma chambre** = I brought down the book from my room and **J'ai sorti la voiture du garage** = I took the car out of the garage.

**La clé** = the key. **Clé** is an alternative spelling for **clef**.

Notice the spelling of **bagages**, as baggage has an extra 'g' in English.

**C'est bien toi!** = Is it really you! Using **bien** like this is a way of confirming that you are right about something, e.g. **C'est bien le train de Paris?** = Is this the right train for Paris?

**Tu vis** = "you live" from the verb **vivre**.

**Tu vis toujours à Genève**? = Do you still live in Geneva? **Toujours** sometimes has the meaning of "always" e.g. **Je dîne toujours à huit heures** = I always dine at eight o'clock.

### DIALOGUE B

Pierre has finally brought together his four old friends, Jacques, Joseph, Liliane and Martine.

**Un petit rat** was the name given to ballerinas at the Opera house.

**Se marier** = to get married. This is a kind of verb called a reflexive verb that you will be learning about in Unit 14.

Here, **Je me suis mariée** = I got married.

**Le béton** = concrete. Jacques has his head in concrete rather than in the clouds because, as an architect, he must be concerned with the construction of buildings.

**Chouette** is a colloquial word meaning "lovely, great, wonderful".

**Ensemble** is invariable and so does not end in **s**.

**Il manque quelqu'un** = someone is missing. **Il manque** is one of the impersonal verbs like **il faut** that are often used in French.

1. **Elle avait laissé** = she had left.

*Page 131*

5. Listen to the intonation when expressing surprise.

6. **Prendre place** = to take a seat.

# UNIT 14 Histoires vraies

**Skills**
- recounting events

**Grammar**
- Reflexive verbs
- the recent past: **venir de** + infinitive
- **être en train de**
- **depuis**
- the relative pronoun **qui**

**Vocabulary**
- free time
- description of a flat

*Page 132*

**Un parc** can be a large private garden, as in **le château dans son parc**, it can be a **jardin public** or park in a town, or it can be a larger **parc naturel** where plants grow freely and animals roam.

**compter** usually means "to count" but here **La France compte...** = France has/possesses...

**accueillir** which is conjugated in the present tense like a regular **-er** verb means "to welcome".

*Page 133*

There are many properties or **gîtes** to be rented for holidays in France. There are many Agencies both in France and Britain which specialise in this kind of work. They offer properties of all sizes in different locations and cover a wide range of prices.

**Je viens de le louer** = I have just rented it.

**en montagne** = in the mountains; **un studio** = a self-contained (one-roomed) flatlet; **1 300 francs la semaine** = 1,300 francs per week; **un acompte** = a deposit.

*Page 134*

**Les classes de neige.** Skiing tuition combined with lessons was originally offered by the state to classes of children from schools in inner cities and underprivileged areas but it has extended to children from all kinds of schools. The morning is spent in the classroom with the usual teacher, the afternoon on the ski slopes.

**Les élèves ...étaient en classe de neige....depuis une semaine** = The pupils had been skiing for a week.

**Le moniteur** = the instructor.

Reflexive verbs in this passage are **se promener** (to go for a walk), **s'inquiéter** (to get worried), **se perdre** (to get lost), **se rappeler** (to remember) and **s'installer** (to settle down).

There are many dangers in the high mountain ranges in France. Apart from skiing accidents, there are avalanches, snowstorms and rapidly changing conditions which give plenty of work to the rescue workers (**les secouristes**).

*Page 135*

**Un immeuble** = a building or block of flats; **en location** = to rent.

The **studio** is one large room divided by partition walls. **la baignoire** = bathtub; **le coin séjour** = living room section; **se reposer** = to rest; **se baigner** = to bathe.

*Page 136*

The relative pronoun **qui** meaning "who" or "which" refers to the subject of the verb e.g. **Il y a beaucoup de touristes qui visitent la région.** It is the tourists who are doing the visiting.

**Reflexive verbs**

Although many verbs are used reflexively in English (to wash oneself, to dress oneself etc.) reflexive verbs are used much more often in French. The only difference from other verbs is the presence of the reflexive pronouns which refer back to the subject of the verb. Hence **je me lave, tu te laves, il se lave** etc. You have already met **me, te, nous** and **vous** as subject or object pronouns, so **se** is the only unfamiliar pronoun.

Note the imperative forms, which unlike those of other verbs, are followed by a pronoun - **lave-toi, lavons-nous** and **lavez-vous.**

Note the position of the reflexive pronouns in the present and perfect tenses and also with the negative.

Notice, too, the agreement of the past participle.

Many verbs can be used as reflexive verbs when the action refers back to the subject or as ordinary verbs when the action is done to another person or thing. Look at the examples of this at the bottom of the page.

*Page 137*

**The recent past**

The construction **venir de + infinitive** means "to have just done something" and is formed from the present tense of the verb **venir** = "to come" followed by an infinitive, e.g. **Je viens de me lever** = I have just got up; **Nous venons de nous promener** = we have just been for a walk.

Remember that **venir + infinitive** can be used with the meaning of coming to do something e.g. **Viens voir** = come and see or **Le garçon vient apporter les boissons** = the waiter is coming to bring the drinks.

### The present

As there is no present continuous tense in French corresponding to the English **I am singing, you are singing** etc. the construction **être en train de + infinitive** is extremely useful. Like **venir de** it can be used in any person, e.g. **Il est en train de chanter** = He is singing or **Vous êtes en train de chanter** = you are singing.

*Page 138*

**DIALOGUE A**

**Quelle rigolade!** = What a laugh/fun!

**la colo** = short for **la colonie de vacances**.

**une course** is "a race" so **la course au trésor** is "a treasure hunt".

**faire équipe avec** = to be in the same team as.

**chacun** = each one; **tout à l'heure** = shortly, presently. Used with a verb in the past **tout à l'heure** can mean "a short time ago" or "just now".

**DIALOGUE B**

**essaient** - The **y** of **essayer** has changed into an **i** because the ending **-ent** is not pronounced.

**La Joconde** is the famous portrait of the Mona Lisa, painted by Leonardo da Vinci, which hangs in the museum of Le Louvre in Paris.

*Page 139*

6. **Rêveur** = dreamy is one of the family of words, including **un rêve** = a dream and **rêver** = to dream and **une rêverie** = day dreaming.

*Pages 140 and 141*

**Bilan**

2. Note that **un photographe** = a photographer and **une photographie** = a photograph.

**Un(e) critique** = a critic but **Une critique** also means "an appreciation" or "criticism".

3. **prendre feu** = to catch fire; **un rescapé** = a survivor.

4. More reflexive verbs: **s'habiller** = to get dressed; **se coucher** = to lie down or go to bed; **s'embrasser** = to kiss; **le sapin** = the fir tree.

12. **embaucher** = to take on (staff).

# UNIT 15 Une journée à Paris

**Skills**
- asking for/giving/understanding information on journeys
- talking about the place where you live

**Grammar**
- the pronouns **y** and **en**
  **bien, mieux, bon, meilleur**
- **oui** and **si**

**Vocabulary**
- monuments
- finding your way about
- giving measurements

*Page 142*

**La tour Eiffel** was built by an engineer called Gustave Eiffel for the Universal Exhibition in 1889. In the spring of 1997 a large electronic clock was placed halfway up the tower to count down the last 1000 days before the millennium.

**la rouille** = rust

**La Pyramide du Louvre**, designed by the Chinese born American architect, Ieoh Ming Po, and opened in 1989, ready for the two hundredth anniversary of the Louvre in 1993, is now the main entrance to the museum. The glass construction, whose exterior is cleaned every three weeks, is intended to reflect the changing colours of the sky over Paris. Like some of the other monuments commissioned by French presidents to enrich the national heritage, the Pyramid is admired by some and disliked by others. The latest of these buildings to be inaugurated was **La Bibliothèque Nationale** in 1996. You can see this on page 158.

*Page 143*

**Un alpiniste** = a mountaineer; **Qu'est-ce qui se passe?** = What is happening?.

The plural of **le travail** is **les travaux; un ouvrier** = a workman;

**les carreaux** = the (window) panes; **plaisanter** = to joke.

**Ils nettoient**. The **y** of **nettoyer** has changed into an **i** because of the silent ending **-ent**.

*Page 144*

**Habiter en banlieue =** Living in the suburbs.

It is interesting to compare the views of these suburban dwellers on their life with the opinion expressed in the phrase **métro, boulot, dodo**, meaning that all there is time for is going to work on the metro, working and sleeping.

**Le 14e** = the 14th arrondissement or postal district of Paris. See the plan on page 158.

**Se distraire** = to enjoy oneself; **s'énerver** = to fret, get upset; **être de mauvaise humeur** = to be in a bad mood.

*Page 145*

**Measurements.**

Remember that **large** means wide and that **long** needs a **u** before the **e** in the feminine form, in order to keep the **g** soft.

**Long** becomes **longue**.

**Les transports en commun** = Public transport. The same tickets are used on the buses as on the metro.

*Page 146*

The pronoun **y** has several meanings in English, "there" or "in that place" or "to it" and the pronoun **en** can mean "some" or "of it" or "of them". Study the examples given in which **y** replace **à, en, dans, sur,** and **en** replaces **de** before a noun, except for a proper noun. Note the position of **y** and **en** after a positive command - **allons-y, sortons-en** and also the **s** added to the second person singular of the positive command, when it is followed by **y** or **en: - vas-y, parles-en.**

*Page 147*

The adjective "good" is **bon (un bon restaurant)**, the comparative of **bon** is **meilleur (un meilleur restaurant)**. Remember to make the adjective agree with the noun it describes, e.g. a better house is **une meilleure maison**.

The adverb "well" is **bien (On mange bien au restaurant)** and the comparative of **bien** is **mieux (on mange mieux à la maison)**. The adverb does not agree with the verb it qualifies.

Use **si** instead of **oui** or **non**, when you disagree with a negative question, e.g. **Vous n'êtes pas anglais? Si, je suis anglais.** You do not agree that you are not English.

*Page 148*

**DIALOGUE A**

**autrefois** = formerly; **rigolo** = funny; **une marche** = a step.

**La Grande Arche** is the latest triumphal arch to be built by the French. This one is in a straight line going west from **L'arc de Triomphe de l'Étoile** in the district of **La Défense**, just past Neuilly. **Les Puces** is **Le marché aux Puces** or second hand market at St-Ouen, near the Porte de Clignancourt, in the north of Paris. This is the most popular of the flea markets and attracts about 150,000 visitors every year. It sells furniture, paintings, books, china and jewellery. **Montmartre**, which was an independent village until it became part of Paris in 1860 is the hill on which stands **La basilique du Sacré-Coeur**. **La Place du Tertre** is the artistic quarter near the **Sacré-Coeur** where artists compete to paint the portraits of tourists and sell their paintings.

*Page 149*

**DIALOGUE B**

5. You may already have visited or have heard about some of these places in Paris.

**Le Moulin Rouge** was the famous night spot in Montmartre, where the artist Toulouse Lautrec painted so many dancers.

**La Sorbonne** is the oldest part of the University of Paris, founded in the Middle Ages by Michel de Sorbon.

**L'Orangerie**, which was a conservatory for growing oranges, built as an annexe to the Louvre, is now an art gallery.

**Le Châtelet** is now a large undergound station under the site of a former fortress in the centre of Paris.

**Picasso** is a famous Spanish painter, who died in 1973.

# UNIT 16 Dénouement

**Skills**
- telling a story in the past

**Grammar**
- the verbs **croire** and **apercevoir**
- revision of past tenses and use of personal pronouns
- plural of nouns

**Vocabulary**
- describing someone's character
- building up the sequence of events in a story

*Page 150*

**Apercevoir** = to notice (with the eyes); **s'apercevoir** = to realise (in the mind); **la cave** = the cellar; **un sac-poubelle** = a dustbin bag; **le coffre** = the boot (of car).

Look carefully at the verb tenses used in this text and differentiate between the use of the Perfect and the Imperfect.

*Page 151*

**Le squelette** = the skeleton.

Notice the position of **tout** in **J'ai tout raconté. D'après lui** = in his view, according to him.

**On est entrés** = We entered. As the indefinite pronoun **on** is used instead of the plural pronoun "we", the past participle agrees with a masculine plural subject.

**Sans** = without. **Sans lune** = without a moon and **sans faire de bruit** = without making any noise. The verb following **sans** must always be in the infinitive.

**En bas** = downstairs, down below; **en haut** = upstairs, up above.

*Page 152*

The next day can be translated by **le lendemain** or **le jour suivant**. **La fête foraine** = the travelling fair; **le train fantôme** = the ghost train; **un virage** = a bend; **barrer la route** = to bar the way, block the road; **la sorcière** = witch; **le costume** = (man's) suit; **faire noir** = to be dark.

*Page 153*

**Une histoire policière** = a detective story;

1. **mince** = slim; **une relation** = an acquaintance.

2. **le jour d'avant/la veille** = the day before; **tout à coup** = suddenly.

4. **un schéma** = a plan

*Page 154*

**croire** can mean to believe or to think. **Croire que...** = to think/believe that...(the word "that" is sometimes omitted in English but **que** can never be omitted in French when it introduces a subordinate clause. **croire** can be followed by an infinitve, e.g. **J'ai cru apercevoir un fantôme** = I thought I had seen a ghost.

*Page 155*

4. **Un film qui passait à la télévision** = a film that was being shown on television.

THE PLURAL OF NOUNS

A noun which ends in **s** or **x** does not change in the plural (**des mois, des prix**) Some masculine nouns that end in **-eau** and **-eu** add **x** for the plural (**des bureaux, des lieux**) as do those ending in **-al** (des **animaux**) but some nouns ending in **-al** add **s** to form the plural (**des festivals**).

*Page 156*

**DIALOGUE A**

The much heralded meeting between the five old friends finally takes place at La Pyramide du Louvre.

When the adjective **ancien** follows the noun it describes, it has the meaning of "old" or "ancient", as in **un jeu de cartes ancien**, but when it is placed before the noun, it has the meaning of "former", e.g. **mon ancien ami** = my former friend.

Card playing is a popular activity in France. Regular customers in small cafés and bars can often be seen playing cards, sometimes with **le patron**.

**Un farceur** = a joker.

**Un collectionneur** = a collector. Many French people enjoy collecting all kinds of things, from antiques to **les pins** (lapel badges).

**DIALOGUE B**

**Ramasser** = to pick up; **une péniche** = a barge; **avoir l'air** = to look (like).

**L'orchestre** could be a symphony orchestra or a small group or band of musicians.

*Page 157*

4. **une montre** = a watch; **une bague** = a ring; **de la vaisselle** = crockery

5. **Comme ils ont l'air heureux!** = How happy they look!

## PARIS, CAPITALE

The plan of Paris is known as the **escargot**, as the number 1 arrondissement begins in the centre and spirals round in a snail shape. You will notice that most of the prestigious monuments shown are in the central or western part of the city. The siting of the **Bibliothèque nationale** in the eastern part of Paris was a deliberate attempt to give life to the poorer side of the city.

Some of the new buildings have proved very costly to the state and some, like the **opéra Bastille**, have already shown faults in construction or design.

There has been concern about storing the nation's books in the high towers of the new library as the many windows are exposed to the sun.

Whatever the problems, there is no doubt about the adventurous, innovative nature of the new Paris buildings and the popularity of Paris with the world's tourists. It is, in fact, the most visited capital in the world.

**artisanal** = craft; **le tissu** = cloth.

The chart shows clearly the supreme importance of the capital in the economic life of the country.

**La Pentecôte** = Whitsuntide; **compte tenu que…**= taking into account.

You will see that French people do not set a letter out in the same way as English people. Firstly, the name and address of the sender is written on the left-hand side of the page and the name and address of the recipient on the right-hand side of the page.

The name of the sender's town precedes the date at the top of the letter.

The French equivalent of "Dear Sir" is **Monsieur**, "Dear Sirs" is **Messieurs**, and "Dear Madam" is **Madame.**

There are many different French versions of "Yours faithfully", some of them being considerably longer than the ones suggested on this page. **Veuillez agréer, monsieur/messieurs/madame, l'expression de nos sentiments les plus distingués** is a favourite ending to a formal letter.

# PRÉCIS GRAMMATICAL

# SOS grammaire

**s'accorder (avec):** to agree with.

**(Un) adjectif:** an adjective is a word that describes a noun or pronoun.

- **qualificatif:** a descriptive adjective indicates a quality, tells what kind it is: **un livre intéressant, il est vieux.**

- **démonstratif:** a demonstrative adjective points out someone or something and distinguishes between things: in English, "this" or "that". In French, it changes with number and gender: **ce** livre, **cette table, ces chaises.**

- **interrogatif:** an interrogative adjective asks a question about someone or something: **Quelle heure est-il? Quel fromage mangez- vous?**

- **possessif:** a possessive adjective shows possession, it tells whose it is. In French it changes with number and gender as well as person: **mon frère**, **ma soeur**, **mes parents.**

- **(un) adjectif / adverbe comparatif:** comparative adjectives show how things relate to each other, "more / less expensive" = **plus / moins cher**: comparative adverbs are also introduced by **plus / moins: plus vite / moins bien.** There are exceptions.

**(un) adverbe:** an adverb is a word that describes a verb, an adjective or another adverb: **je cours vite, il mange peu.**

**article:** goes before a noun to explain its status -

- **défini:** definite, for specific things: **le téléphone, les enfants.**

- **indéfini:** indefinite; **un jean, une robe, des vêtements** (clothes - "some" often omitted in English).

**(le) complément:** object. Transitive verbs need an object to complete their meaning.

**direct:** noun or pronoun that receives directly the action of the verb.

**indirect:** noun or pronoun that receives the action of the verb indirectly with the preposition to relate it to the verb.

**circonstanciel**; adverbial phrase of time or place.

**(une) conjugaison:** conjugation - a group of verbs of a particular form, e.g. the **-er** verbs, like **parler**.

**(une) consonne:** consonant; all the letters which are not vowels.

**(le) déterminant:** the determiner, i.e. what decides.

**(le) genre:** gender, i.e. masculine or feminine.

**(un) impératif:** imperative: part of the verb which gives orders.

**l'indicatif:** indicative; normal use of the verb, as compared to the subjunctive.

**l'infinitif:** infinitive; the basic form of the verb, like "to do" or "to have".

**(une) locution:** phrase or idiom.

**muet:** mute; not pronounced.

**(le) nom:** noun; a word that can be the name of a person, animal, place, thing, event or idea.

- **propre:** proper: a proper noun names a specific person, place or thing.

**(un) nombre:** number; whether one (singular) or more (plural) are involved.

**(l') orthographe:** spelling.

**(un) participe passé:** past participle; form of the verb used with an auxiliary verb to indicate the perfect tense: **J'ai parlé.**

**(une) personne:** person; the first person is the person speaking, **je** is singular and **nous** is plural; the second person is the person spoken to, **tu** is singular and **vous** is plural;

the third person is the person spoken about, **il** and **elle** are singular and **ils** and **elles** are plural.

**(une) phrase:** sentence or phrase.

- **affirmative**: expresses a fact or situation that is.

- **auxiliaire**: auxiliary; helps another verb to form one of its tenses..

- **négative**: expresses a fact or situation that is not.

- **subordonnée**: when there are two or more parts to a sentence, only one will make sense on its own. This is called the main clause, and the other parts are called subordinate.

**pluriel**: plural; more than one.

**(une) préposition**: preposition; a word that shows the relationship of one word (usually a noun or a pronoun) to another word in the sentence e.g. **le chien est <u>dans</u> le jardin, Jean est <u>à côté de</u> moi.**

**(un) pronom**: pronoun; a word used in place of one or more nouns in order to avoid repeating the noun(s). **Lucie est grande. <u>Elle</u> est mince aussi.**

- **indéfini**: indefinite; relates to unidentified persons or things, e.g. **on**

- **personnel**: personal; relates to a person or animal, **je, tu, il** etc.

- **tonique**: emphatic; **moi, toi, lui** etc.

**(le) radical**: the stem of the verb, which does not usually change and to which endings are added, e.g. **nous <u>parl</u>-ons**.

**singulier**: singular, only one.

**(le) sujet**: subject; the person or thing that performs the action.

**(la) syllabe**: syllable.

**(le) temps**: tense; indicates the time when the action of the verb takes place.

- **présent**: present; the action is taking place now.

- **passé composé**: perfect; a completed action in the past.

- **imparfait**: imperfect; an action that was continuous or repeated, that was going on in the past.

- **futur simple**: future; the action will take place in the future.

- **futur proche**: immediate future, what is going to happen.

**(le) verbe**: verb; indicates the action of a sentence, **je joue au foot** or a state **je suis fatigué**.

- **pronominal**: reflexive; a verb that is linked to a special pronoun called a reflexive pronoun, **me, te, se, nous, vous**, which reflects the action of the verb back to the performer, that is, the subject of the sentence.

**(une) voyelle**: vowel, the letters a, e, i, o and u.

# PRÉCIS GRAMMATICAL

*Use the SOS Grammaire to help you understand the grammatical terms.*

## LA PHRASE SIMPLE ────────────────────────

### ▪ LA PHRASE AFFIRMATIVE

**1. Sujet + verbe**

> *Je sors.*
> *Les enfants dorment.*

**2. Sujet + verbe + complément direct ou indirect**

- **Il n'y a pas de préposition** entre le verbe et le complément direct.
  *Florence lit le journal.*

- **Il y a une préposition** (**à** ou **de**) entre le verbe et le complément indirect.
  *Claire téléphone **à** son ami.*
  *Tout le monde parle **de** ce film.*

**3. Sujet + verbe + adjectif ou nom**

> *Béatrice est **grande**.*
> *Florence est **pilote**.*

**4. Sujet + verbe + complément circonstanciel**

> Le complément circonstanciel indique le lieu, le temps, le but…
> Sa place est variable dans la phrase.
> *Ils travaillent **au Canada*** = complément de lieu.
> ***Pendant les vacances**, je fais de la randonnée* = complément de temps.

# ■ LA PHRASE INTERROGATIVE

## 1. L'interrogation totale

Elle porte sur toute la phrase. La réponse est **oui** ou **non**.

On emploie :

- **l'intonation** (la voix monte en fin de phrase)

    *Tu as fini ?*

    *Il fait froid ?*

- **est-ce que**

    *Est-ce que tu as fini ?*

    *Est-ce qu'il fait froid ?*

 Si la question est négative, la réponse n'est pas oui mais **si**.

*Tu ne viens pas avec nous au cinéma ?*      ***Si**, je viens.*

## 2. L'interrogation partielle

Elle porte sur une partie de la phrase :

- sur le **sujet**

    *Le dimanche, **Richard** joue au foot.* ➜ ***Qui** joue au foot ?*

- sur le **complément direct**

    *J'ai acheté **deux disques**.* ➜ ***Qu'est-ce que** tu as acheté ?*

- sur le **complément indirect**

    *Elle téléphone **à son ami**.* ➜ *Elle téléphone **à qui** ?*

- sur le **complément circonstanciel**

    *Le train part **à 20h 05**.* ➜ *Le train part **quand** ?*

### Les différents types d'interrogation partielle

| | question avec intonation | question avec est-ce que |
|---|---|---|
| sujet | **Qui** est là ? | **Qui est-ce qui** est là ? |
| complément direct | Vous voulez **quoi** ? | **Qu'est-ce que** vous voulez ? |
| complément indirect | **À qui** tu écris ? | **À qui est-ce que** tu écris ? |
| complément circonstanciel | | |
| de lieu | Vous habitez **où** ? | **Où est-ce que** vous habitez ? |
| de temps | Ils partent **quand** ? | **Quand est-ce qu'**ils partent ? |
| | Vous partez **à quelle heure** ? | **À quelle heure est-ce que** vous partez ? |
| de but | Vous travaillez **pour qui** ? | **Pour qui est-ce que** vous travaillez ? |
| de manière | Elle va à Lyon **comment** ? | **Comment est-ce qu'**elle va à Lyon ? |
| de cause | **Pourquoi** elle rit ? | **Pourquoi est-ce qu'**elle rit ? |
| de prix | Ça coûte **combien** ? | **Combien est-ce que** ça coûte ? |

 Pour les compléments indirects et les compléments circonstanciels, le mot interrogatif se place au début ou à la fin de la phrase.

*À qui tu écris ? Tu écris à qui ?*

*Combien ça coûte ? Ça coûte combien ?*

# ■ LA PHRASE NÉGATIVE

## 1. La négation du verbe

- **ne (n') ... pas**

    *Il **ne** pleut **pas**.*

    *Elle **n'**aime **pas** danser.*

     Au **passé composé**, on emploie :

    **ne + auxiliaire + pas + participe passé.**

    *Il **n'**a **pas** répondu.*

    Avec les **verbes pronominaux**, on emploie :

    **ne + pronom + verbe (ou auxiliaire) + pas.**

    *Elle **ne** se promène **pas**.*

    *Elle **ne** s'est **pas** promenée.*

- **ne ... jamais**

    *– Vous regardez toujours / souvent la télévision le soir ?*

    *– Non, je **ne** regarde **jamais** la télévision le soir.*

- **ne ... plus**

    *– Vous habitez toujours / encore à Aix ?*

    *– Non, je **n'**habite **plus** à Aix (avant j'y habitais).*

- **ne ... pas encore**

    *– Tu as déjà vu ce film ?*

    *– Non, je **n'**ai **pas encore** vu ce film (je le verrai peut-être).*

## 2. La négation du complément direct, précédé de l'article indéfini ou de l'article partitif

- **ne ... pas / ne ... jamais / ne ... plus + de**

    *J'ai **une** voiture.*            *Je **n'**ai **pas de** voiture.*

    *Elle a acheté **des** fruits.*        *Elle **n'**a **pas** acheté **de** fruits.*

    *Il boit **de la** bière.*           *Il **ne** boit **jamais de** bière.*

    *Pierre fait **du** sport.*          *Pierre **ne** fait **plus de** sport.*

## 3. La négation du pronom indéfini

- **personne ... ne**

    *– Quelqu'un a téléphoné ?*

    *– Non, **personne n'**a téléphoné.*

- **ne ... rien**

    *– Vous voulez quelque chose à boire ?*

    *– Non merci, je **ne** veux **rien**.*

    *– Vous avez tout compris ?*

    *– Non, je **n'**ai **rien** compris.*

# LE GROUPE DU NOM

## ■ LE NOM

### 1. Genre du nom

Un nom est masculin ou féminin : *un livre, une table.*
En général, on ajoute un **-e** à la forme du masculin pour former le féminin des noms de personnes.

- **La prononciation peut rester la même.**

  *un ami*                    *une amie*

- **La prononciation peut changer : on entend la consonne finale.**

  *un marchand*        *une marchande*
  *un infirmier*         *une infirmière*
  *un Japonais*         *une Japonaise*
  *un voisin*             *une voisine*
  *un informaticien*    *une informaticienne*

- **La syllabe finale peut être modifiée.**

  *un serveur*          *une serveuse*
  *un acteur*           *une actrice*
  *un sportif*          *une sportive*

- **Beaucoup de noms terminés par -e sont masculin ou féminin. C'est le déterminant qui indique le genre.**

  *un / une artiste*
  *un / une architecte*

### 2. Nombre du nom

Un nom est singulier ou pluriel : *la maison, les maisons.*
En général, on ajoute un **-s** à la forme du singulier pour former le pluriel.

- **Il n'y a pas de changement pour les noms terminés par -s.**

  *le mois*              *les mois*
  *le pays*              *les pays*

- **On ajoute un -x aux noms terminés par -eau ou -eu.**

  *le bureau*          *les bureaux*
  *le lieu*             *les lieux*

- **Les noms terminés en -al ont un pluriel en -aux.**

  *le journal*         *les journaux*

Exception : le festival, les festivals.

- **Pluriels irréguliers.**

  *un œil*               *des yeux*
  *un jeune homme*       *des jeunes gens*
  *madame*               *mesdames*
  *monsieur*             *messieurs*
  *mademoiselle*         *mesdemoiselles*

# ◼ LE DÉTERMINANT

Un nom est généralement précédé d'un déterminant.

## 1. L'article

|  | singulier | | pluriel |
|---|---|---|---|
|  | **masculin** | **féminin** |  |
| **indéfini** | un | une | des |
| **défini** | le / l' | la / l' | les |
| **partitif** | du / de l' | de la / de l' | des |

## 2. L'adjectif démonstratif

|  | **masculin** | **féminin** |
|---|---|---|
| **singulier** | ce / cet | cette |
| **pluriel** | ces | |

## 3. L'adjectif possessif

|  | **masculin** | **féminin** |
|---|---|---|
| **singulier** | mon, ton, son | ma, ta, sa |
|  | notre, votre, leur | |
| **pluriel** | mes, tes, ses, nos, vos, leurs | |

## 4. L'adjectif interrogatif

|  | **masculin** | **féminin** |
|---|---|---|
| **singulier** | quel | quelle |
| **pluriel** | quels | quelles |

# ◼ L'ADJECTIF QUALIFICATIF

L'adjectif qualificatif s'accorde avec le nom. Il peut être masculin ou féminin, singulier ou pluriel.

*un manteau noir*
*une petite fille*
*des fruits sucrés*
*des étudiantes italiennes*

## 1. Genre de l'adjectif qualificatif

Pour former le féminin des adjectifs à l'écrit, on ajoute un **-e** au masculin.

**• La prononciation peut rester la même.**

| | |
|---|---|
| *normal* | *normale* |
| *exceptionnel* | *exceptionnelle* |
| *cher* | *chère* |
| *grec* | *grecque* |
| *jeune* | *jeune* |

**Attention à l'orthographe.**

- **La prononciation peut changer.**

| | | |
|---|---|---|
| grand | grande | |
| chinois | chinoise | |
| bon | bonne | |
| gros | grosse | **La consonne finale** |
| étranger | étrangère | **est prononcée.** |
| complet | complète | |
| voisin | voisine | |
| sportif | sportive | |
| heureux | heureuse | **La consonne finale** |
| blanc | blanche | **est modifiée.** |
| doux | douce | |

- **Cas particuliers : beau, nouveau, vieux.**

| | |
|---|---|
| beau | belle |
| nouveau | nouvelle |
| vieux | vieille |

Devant un nom masculin commençant par une **voyelle** ou un **h muet**, beau devient **bel**, nouveau devient **nouvel**, vieux devient **vieil**.

| | |
|---|---|
| un beau pays | un bel appartement |
| un nouveau restaurant | un nouvel hôpital |
| un vieux quartier | un vieil hôtel |

## 2. Nombre de l'adjectif qualificatif

Pour former le pluriel des adjectifs à l'écrit, on ajoute un **-s** à la forme masculine ou féminine du singulier.

| | |
|---|---|
| joli | joli**s**, joli**es** |
| grand | grand**s**, grand**es** |

Les adjectifs masculins terminés par **-eau** ou **-al** ont un pluriel en **-x**.

| | |
|---|---|
| beau | beau**x** |
| national | nationau**x** |

## 3. Place de l'adjectif qualificatif

En général, l'adjectif se place après le nom.

*un repas excellent, des étudiants grecs, une robe verte*

Les adjectifs **bon, beau, joli, petit, grand, gros, mauvais, nouveau, prochain, premier, dernier** se placent avant le nom.

*un joli tableau,*
*le premier étage,*
*un gros gâteau*

# LE PRONOM PERSONNEL _____

Un pronom se met à la place d'un nom.

## 1. Les pronoms des première et deuxième personnes

|  | singulier | | pluriel | |
|---|---|---|---|---|
|  | **je** | **tu** | **nous** | **vous** |
| **complément direct et indirect** | me / m' | te / t' | nous | vous |
| **tonique ou après une préposition** | moi | toi | nous | vous |

## 2. Les pronoms de la troisième personne

|  | singulier | | pluriel | |
|---|---|---|---|---|
|  | **il** | **elle** | **ils** | **elles** |
| **complément direct** | le / l' | la / l' | les | |
| **complément indirect** | lui | | leur | |
| **tonique ou après une préposition** | lui | elle | eux | elles |

- Complément direct

    *Florence **me** regarde.*

    *Il **la** regarde.*

- Complément indirect

    *Florence **me** parle.*

    *Il **lui** parle.*

- Pronom tonique

    ***Moi**, j'adore la musique.*

    *Les garçons, **eux**, aiment le foot mais les filles, **elles**, préfèrent la danse.*

- Pronom après une préposition

    *Thierry travaille avec **moi**.*

    *Je travaille pour **lui** depuis deux ans.*

## 3. En et y

- **En,** pronom, remplace un groupe nominal précédé de la préposition **de**.

    *Vous parlez de vos prochaines vacances.* ➜ *Vous **en** parlez.*

    *Vous prenez un kilo de pommes.* ➜ *Vous **en** prenez un kilo.*

- **Y,** remplace un groupe nominal précédé de la préposition **à**, **en**, **dans**, **sur**, etc.

    *– Tu vas souvent à la campagne ? – Oui, j'**y** vais souvent.*

    *– Vous vous intéressez au cinéma ? – Oui, je m'**y** intéresse.*

# LE VERBE

## ■ EMPLOI DES TEMPS DE L'INDICATIF

### 1. Le présent

- Action en cours
  *Les gens **se promènent** dans le jardin.*
- Action dans un futur très proche
  *Je **reviens** dans cinq minutes.*
- Action habituelle
  *Les enfants **prennent** quatre repas par jour.*
- Vérité générale
  *La neige **est** blanche.*

### 2. Le futur simple

- Événement probable
  *Il **pleuvra** demain.*

### 3. L'imparfait

- Circonstances, état, action en cours
  *Je **regardais** la télévision quand Luc m'a téléphoné.*
- Description
  *C'**était** une journée magnifique : le ciel **était** bleu, le soleil **brillait**.*
- Action habituelle
  *Quand nous **habitions** à Paris, nous **allions** souvent à l'Opéra.*

### 4. Le passé composé

- Action terminée
  *Ils **ont acheté** leur maison en 1992.*
- Succession d'actions
  *Les touristes **ont visité** le Louvre, ils **sont montés** à la tour Eiffel, puis ils se **sont promenés** dans le quartier du Marais.*

### 5. Emplois particuliers

- **Être en train de + infinitif :** une action en cours d'accomplissement
  *Elle **est en train d'**écrire une lettre.*
- **Aller + infinitif :** le futur proche, une action proche et considérée comme certaine
  *Je **vais acheter** une voiture.*
- **Venir de + infinitif :** le passé récent, une action passée très proche
  *Je **viens de rencontrer** Béatrice dans la rue.*

# ■ CONJUGAISONS

## 1. Les verbes être et avoir

Ils servent à former les temps composés. Ce sont des auxiliaires.

*Elle a accompagné son fils à la gare.*

*Je suis sorti hier.*

Ils sont aussi employés comme des verbes.

*Mes amis ont une maison avec un jardin.*

*Françoise est très jolie.*

## 2. Les trois groupes de verbes

• **Premier groupe : infinitif en -er** (donner, parler, etc.)

90% des verbes sont des verbes du premier groupe.

Le radical est le même à tous les temps.

*je **donn**e, il **donn**ait, tu as **donn**é*

• **Deuxième groupe : infinitif en -ir** (finir, choisir, etc.)

Le radical ne change pas, mais l'élément **-iss** apparaît à certains temps.

*je **fin**is, je **fin**issais*

• **Troisième groupe : quelques verbes irréguliers très fréquents**

Le radical est variable.

Verbes en **-ir** : venir, partir, etc.

*je viens, je pars.*

Verbes en **-re** : faire, prendre, etc.

*je fais, nous prenons.*

Verbes en **-oir** : pouvoir, savoir, etc.

*je peux, je sais.*

## 3. Remarques générales sur les temps de l'indicatif

• **Le présent**

On entend la consonne finale du radical pour les verbes des 1er et 2e groupes.

*par**l**er → je par**l**e*            *fin**ir** → il fin**it***

On n'entend pas la consonne finale du radical pour de nombreux verbes
du 3e groupe.

*sor**t**ir → je sors*            *descen**d**re → je descends*

• **L'imparfait**

Il est toujours formé sur le radical de la première personne du pluriel du présent
(sauf pour le verbe être).

Les terminaisons sont les mêmes pour tous les verbes.

*nous **parl**ons    →  je parl**ais***

*nous **finiss**ons →  je finiss**ais***

*nous **écriv**ons →  nous écriv**ions***

### • Le futur simple

Il est toujours formé sur l'infinitif du verbe.

Les terminaisons sont les mêmes pour tous les verbes.

*donner* ➜ *je donner**ai***

*choisir* ➜ *je choisir**ai***

Quelques verbes du troisième groupe ont un futur irrégulier.

*faire* ➜ *je ferai*      *aller* ➜ *j'irai*      *voir* ➜ *je verrai*

### • Le passé composé

En général, le passé composé se forme avec **l'auxiliaire avoir**.

*J'**ai** téléphoné.*

 Les verbes **aller, arriver, descendre, entrer, monter, mourir, naître, passer, rester, retourner, sortir, tomber, venir** se conjuguent avec **l'auxiliaire être**.

*Elle **est** partie très tôt.*

Mais les verbes **descendre, monter, sortir, passer** se conjuguent avec **l'auxiliaire avoir** quand ils sont suivis d'un complément direct.

*Il **a** descendu sa valise. J'**ai** passé une bonne soirée.*

**Les verbes pronominaux** se conjuguent aussi avec l'auxiliaire être.

*Robert s'**est** levé à 7 heures.*

# TABLEAUX DE CONJUGAISONS

**Les verbes du premier groupe en -er : parler**

| indicatif | |
|---|---|
| **présent** | je parl**e** |
| | tu parl**es** |
| | il / elle parl**e** |
| | nous parl**ons** |
| | vous parl**ez** |
| | ils / elles parl**ent** |
| **futur** | je parler**ai** |
| | tu parler**as** |
| | il / elle parler**a** |
| | nous parler**ons** |
| | vous parler**ez** |
| | ils / elles parler**ont** |
| **passé composé** | j'ai parl**é** |
| | tu as parl**é** |
| | il / elle a parl**é** |
| | nous avons parl**é** |
| | vous avez parl**é** |
| | ils / elles ont parl**é** |
| **imparfait** | je parl**ais** |
| | tu parl**ais** |
| | il / elle parl**ait** |
| | nous parl**ions** |
| | vous parl**iez** |
| | ils / elles parl**aient** |

| impératif | |
|---|---|
| **présent** | parl**e** |
| | parl**ons** |
| | parl**ez** |

 Il n'y a pas de **-s** à la 2e personne de l'impératif, sauf quand le verbe est suivi de **en** et **y**.

*Donnes-en !*       *Offres-en !*

**Remarques**

• Attention à la **prononciation** des verbes comme **étudier** : on entend le i du radical.

*j'étudie, ils étudient, vous étudiiez (imparfait)*

• Quelques verbes présentent des **modifications orthographiques**.

– Verbes en **-ger** (changer, manger, voyager, etc.)

Présent : nous mang**e**ons

Imparfait : je mang**e**ais, tu mang**e**ais, etc.

– Verbes comme lever, préférer : **è + e muet**

Présent : je l**è**ve, tu l**è**ves, il l**è**ve, ils l**è**vent

je préf**è**re, tu préf**è**res, il préf**è**re, ils préf**è**rent

– Verbes comme payer, essayer : **y** ou **i + e muet**

Présent : je pa**i**e / je pa**y**e, tu pa**i**es / tu pa**y**es, il pa**i**e / il pa**y**e, ils pa**i**ent / ils pa**y**ent

Futur : je pa**i**erai / je pa**y**erai, tu pa**i**eras / tu pa**y**eras, etc.

– Verbes comme employer, nettoyer : **i + e muet**

Présent : j'emplo**i**e, tu emplo**i**es, il emplo**i**e, ils emplo**i**ent

Futur : j'emplo**i**erai, etc.

exception : envoyer ➜ j'enverrai

– Verbes comme appeler et jeter : **ll** ou **tt + e muet**

| **indicatif** | | |
|---|---|---|
| **présent** | j'appe**ll**e | je je**tt**e |
| | tu appe**ll**es | tu je**tt**es |
| | il / elle appe**ll**e | il / elle je**tt**e |
| | nous appe**l**ons | nous je**t**ons |
| | vous appe**l**ez | vous je**t**ez |
| | ils / elles appe**ll**ent | ils / elles je**tt**ent |
| **futur** | j'appe**ll**erai | je je**tt**erai |
| **passé composé** | j'ai appe**l**é | j'ai je**t**é |

## Les verbes du deuxième groupe en -ir : finir

| **indicatif** | | | |
|---|---|---|---|
| **présent** | je fin**is** | **passé composé** | je finiss**ais** |
| | tu fin**is** | | tu finiss**ais** |
| | il / elle fin**it** | | il / elle finiss**ait** |
| | nous fin**issons** | | nous finiss**ions** |
| | vous fin**issez** | | vous finiss**iez** |
| | ils / elles fin**issent** | | ils / elles finiss**aient** |
| **futur** | je fini**rai** | **imparfait** | j'ai fin**i** |
| | tu fini**ras** | | tu as fin**i** |
| | il / elle fini**ra** | | il / elle a fin**i** |
| | nous fini**rons** | | nous avons fin**i** |
| | vous fini**rez** | | vous avez fin**i** |
| | ils / elles fini**ront** | | ils / elles ont fin**i** |

| **impératif** | |
|---|---|
| **présent** | fin**is** |
| | finiss**ons** |
| | finiss**ez** |

# Les verbes avoir et être

**indicatif**

| **présent** | | |
|---|---|---|
| | j'ai | je suis |
| | tu as | tu es |
| | il / elle a | il / elle est |
| | nous avons | nous sommes |
| | vous avez | vous êtes |
| | ils / elles ont | ils / elles sont |

| **futur** | | |
|---|---|---|
| | j'aurai | je serai |
| | tu auras | tu seras |
| | il / elle aura | il / elle sera |
| | nous aurons | nous serons |
| | vous aurez | vous serez |
| | ils / elles auront | ils / elles seront |

| **imparfait** | | |
|---|---|---|
| | j'avais | j'étais |
| | tu avais | tu étais |
| | il / elle avait | il / elle était |
| | nous avions | nous étions |
| | vous aviez | vous étiez |
| | ils / elles avaient | ils / elles étaient |

| **passé composé** | | |
|---|---|---|
| | j'ai eu | j'ai été |
| | tu as eu | tu as été |
| | il / elle a eu | il / elle a été |
| | nous avons eu | nous avons été |
| | vous avez eu | vous avez été |
| | ils / elles ont eu | ils / elles ont été |

**impératif**

| **présent** | | |
|---|---|---|
| | aie | sois |
| | ayons | soyons |
| | ayez | soyez |

# La conjugaison pronominale

**• Le verbe est précédé d'un pronom de la même personne que le sujet (nom ou pronom).**

je **me** lève

tu **te** lèves

il / elle **se** lève *Paul **se** lève.*

nous **nous** levons

vous **vous** levez

ils / elles **se** lèvent *Les enfants **se** lèvent.*

**• Le passé composé est formé avec l'auxiliaire être. Attention à l'accord du participe passé avec le sujet.**

*Florence s'est habillé**e**.*

*Nous nous sommes promené**(e)s**.*

**• Attention à la place du pronom personnel à l'impératif.**

lève-**toi** ne **te** lève pas

levons-**nous** ne **nous** levons pas

levez-**vous** ne **vous** levez pas

## Les verbes du troisième groupe

| infinitif | indicatif | | | | impératif |
| --- | --- | --- | --- | --- | --- |
| | présent | passé composé | imparfait | futur | présent |
| **aller** | je vais | je suis allé(e) | j'allais | j'irai | |
| | tu vas | tu es allé(e) | tu allais | tu iras | va |
| | il / elle va | il / elle est allé(e) | il / elle allait | il / elle ira | |
| | nous allons | nous sommes allé(e)s | nous allions | nous irons | allons |
| | vous allez | vous êtes allé(e)s | vous alliez | vous irez | allez |
| | ils / elles vont | ils / elles sont allé(e)s | ils / elles allaient | ils / elles iront | |
| **apercevoir** | j'aperçois | j'ai aperçu | j'apercevais | j'apercevrai | |
| recevoir | tu aperçois | tu as aperçu | tu apercevais | tu apercevras | aperçois |
| | il / elle aperçoit | il / elle a aperçu | il / elle apercevait | il / elle apercevra | |
| | nous apercevons | nous avons aperçu | nous apercevions | nous apercevrons | apercevons |
| | vous apercevez | vous avez aperçu | vous aperceviez | vous apercevrez | apercevez |
| | ils / elles aperçoivent | ils / elles ont aperçu | il / elles apercevaient | ils / elles apercevront | |
| **boire** | je bois | j'ai bu | je buvais | je boirai | |
| | tu bois | tu as bu | tu buvais | tu boiras | bois |
| | il / elle boit | il / elle a bu | il / elle buvait | il / elle boira | |
| | nous buvons | nous avons bu | nous buvions | nous boirons | buvons |
| | vous buvez | vous avez bu | vous buviez | vous boirez | buvez |
| | ils / elles boivent | ils / elles ont bu | ils / elles buvaient | ils / elles boiront | |
| **conduire** | je conduis | j'ai conduit | je conduisais | je conduirai | |
| construire | tu conduis | tu as conduit | tu conduisais | tu conduiras | conduis |
| détruire | il / elle conduit | il / elle a conduit | il / elle conduisait | il / elle conduira | |
| introduire | nous conduisons | nous avons conduit | nous conduisions | nous conduirons | conduisons |
| produire | vous conduisez | vous avez conduit | vous conduisiez | vous conduirez | conduisez |
| traduire | ils / elles conduisent | ils / elles ont conduit | ils / elles conduisaient | ils / elles conduiront | |
| **connaître** | je connais | j'ai connu | je connaissais | je connaîtrai | |
| paraître | tu connais | tu as connu | tu connaissais | tu connaîtras | connais |
| disparaître | il / elle connaît | il / elle a connu | il / elle connaissait | il / elle connaîtra | |
| | nous connaissons | nous avons connu | nous connaissions | nous connaîtrons | connaissons |
| | vous connaissez | vous avez connu | vous connaissiez | vous connaîtrez | connaissez |
| | ils / elles connaissent | ils / elles ont connu | ils / elles connaissaient | ils / elles connaîtront | |
| **courir** | je cours | j'ai couru | je courais | je courrai | |
| | tu cours | tu as couru | tu courais | tu courras | cours |
| | il / elle court | il / elle a couru | il / elle courait | il / elle courra | |
| | nous courons | nous avons couru | nous courions | nous courrons | courons |
| | vous courez | vous avez couru | vous couriez | vous courrez | courez |
| | ils / elles courent | ils / elles ont couru | ils / elles couraient | ils / elles courront | |
| **croire** | je crois | j'ai cru | je croyais | je croirai | |
| | tu crois | tu as cru | tu croyais | tu croiras | crois |
| | il / elle croit | il / elle a cru | il / elle croyait | il / elle croira | |
| | nous croyons | nous avons cru | nous croyions | nous croirons | croyons |
| | vous croyez | vous avez cru | vous croyiez | vous croirez | croyez |
| | ils / elles croient | ils / elles ont cru | ils / elles croyaient | ils / elles croiront | |
| **devoir** | je dois | j'ai dû | je devais | je devrai | |
| | tu dois | tu as dû | tu devais | tu devras | |
| | il / elle doit | il / elle a dû | il / elle devait | il / elle devra | |
| | nous devons | nous avons dû | nous devions | nous devrons | |
| | vous devez | vous avez dû | vous deviez | vous devrez | |
| | ils / elles doivent | ils / elles ont dû | ils / elles devaient | ils / elles devront | |
| **dire** | je dis | j'ai dit | je disais | je dirai | |
| interdire | tu dis | tu as dit | tu disais | tu diras | dis |
| | il / elle dit | il / elle a dit | il / elle disait | il / elle dira | |
| | nous disons | nous avons dit | nous disions | nous dirons | disons |
| | vous dites | vous avez dit | vous disiez | vous direz | dites |
| | ils / elles disent | ils / elles ont dit | ils / elles disaient | ils / elles diront | |

| infinitif | indicatif | | | | impératif |
|-----------|-----------|-----------|-----------|-----------|-----------|
| | présent | passé composé | imparfait | futur | présent |
| **dormir** | je dors | j'ai dormi | je dormais | je dormirai | |
| | tu dors | tu as dormi | tu dormais | tu dormiras | dors |
| | il / elle dort | il / elle a dormi | il / elle dormait | il / elle dormira | |
| | nous dormons | nous avons dormi | nous dormions | nous dormirons | dormons |
| | vous dormez | vous avez dormi | vous dormiez | vous dormirez | dormez |
| | ils / elles dorment | ils / elles ont dormi | ils / elles dormaient | ils / elles dormiront | |
| **écrire** | j'écris | j'ai écrit | j'écrivais | j'écrirai | |
| décrire | tu écris | tu as écrit | tu écrivais | tu écriras | écris |
| | il / elle écrit | il / elle a écrit | il / elle écrivait | il / elle écrira | |
| | nous écrivons | nous avons écrit | nous écrivions | nous écrirons | écrivons |
| | vous écrivez | vous avez écrit | vous écriviez | vous écrirez | écrivez |
| | ils / elles écrivent | ils / elles ont écrit | ils / elles écrivaient | ils / elles écriront | |
| **faire** | je fais | j'ai fait | je faisais | je ferai | |
| défaire | tu fais | tu as fait | tu faisais | tu feras | fais |
| refaire | il / elle fait | il / elle a fait | il / elle faisait | il / elle fera | |
| | nous faisons | nous avons fait | nous faisions | nous ferons | faisons |
| | vous faites | vous avez fait | vous faisiez | vous ferez | faites |
| | ils / elles font | ils / elles ont fait | ils / elles faisaient | ils / elles feront | |
| **falloir** | il faut | il a fallu | il fallait | il faudra | |
| **mettre** | je mets | j'ai mis | je mettais | je mettrai | |
| | tu mets | tu as mis | tu mettais | tu mettras | mets |
| | il / elle met | il / elle a mis | ils / elle mettait | il / elle mettra | |
| | nous mettons | nous avons mis | nous mettions | nous mettrons | mettons |
| | vous mettez | vous avez mis | vous mettiez | vous mettrez | mettez |
| | ils / elles mettent | ils / elles ont mis | ils / elles mettaient | ils / elles mettront | |
| **ouvrir** | j'ouvre | j'ai ouvert | j'ouvrais | j'ouvrirai | |
| couvrir | tu ouvres | tu as ouvert | tu ouvrais | tu ouvriras | ouvre |
| découvrir | il / elle ouvre | il / elle a ouvert | il / elle ouvrait | il / elle ouvrira | |
| | nous ouvrons | nous avons ouvert | nous ouvrions | nous ouvrirons | ouvrons |
| | vous ouvrez | vous avez ouvert | vous ouvriez | vous ouvrirez | ouvrez |
| | ils / elles ouvrent | ils / elles ont ouvert | ils / elles ouvraient | ils / elles ouvriront | |
| **partir** | je pars | je suis parti(e) | je partais | je partirai | |
| sortir | tu pars | tu es parti(e) | tu partais | tu partiras | pars |
| | il / elle part | il / elle est parti(e) | il / elle partait | il / elle partira | |
| | nous partons | nous sommes parti(e)s | nous partions | nous partirons | partons |
| | vous partez | vous êtes parti(e)s | vous partiez | vous partirez | partez |
| | ils / elles partent | ils / elles sont parti(e)s | ils / elles partaient | ils / elles partiront | |
| **plaire** | je plais | j'ai plu | je plaisais | je plairai | |
| | tu plais | tu as plu | tu plaisais | tu plairas | plais |
| | il / elle plaît | il / elle a plu | il / elle plaisait | il / elle plaira | |
| | nous plaisons | nous avons plu | nous plaisions | nous plairons | plaisons |
| | vous plaisez | vous avez plu | vous plaisiez | vous plairez | plaisez |
| | ils / elles plaisent | ils / elles ont plu | ils / elles plaisaient | ils / elles plairont | |
| **pleuvoir** | il pleut | il a plu | il pleuvait | il pleuvra | |
| **pouvoir** | je peux | j'ai pu | je pouvais | je pourrai | |
| | tu peux | tu as pu | tu pouvais | tu pourras | |
| | il / elle peut | il / elle a pu | il / elle pouvait | il / elle pourra | |
| | nous pouvons | nous avons pu | nous pouvions | nous pourrons | |
| | vous pouvez | vous avez pu | vous pouviez | vous pourrez | |
| | ils / elles peuvent | ils / elles ont pu | ils / elles pouvaient | ils / elles pourront | |
| **prendre** | je prends | j'ai pris | je prenais | je prendrai | |
| apprendre | tu prends | tu as pris | tu prenais | tu prendras | prends |
| comprendre | il / elle prend | il / elle a pris | il / elle prenait | il / elle prendra | |
| | nous prenons | nous avons pris | nous prenions | nous prendrons | prenons |
| | vous prenez | vous avez pris | vous preniez | vous prendrez | prenez |
| | ils / elles prennent | ils / elles ont pris | ils / elles prenaient | ils / elles prendront | |

| infinitif | indicatif | | | | impératif |
| | présent | passé composé | imparfait | futur | présent |
|---|---|---|---|---|---|
| **rendre**<br>attendre<br>défendre<br>descendre<br>entendre<br>vendre | je rends<br>tu rends<br>il / elle rend<br>nous rendons<br>vous rendez<br>il / elles rendent | j'ai rendu<br>tu as rendu<br>il / elle a rendu<br>nous avons rendu<br>vous avez rendu<br>ils /elles ont rendu | je rendais<br>tu rendais<br>il /elle rendait<br>nous rendions<br>vous rendiez<br>ils / elles rendaient | je rendrai<br>tu rendras<br>il /elle rendra<br>nous rendrons<br>vous rendrez<br>ils /elles rendront | <br>rends<br><br>rendons<br>rendez |
| **répondre** | je réponds<br>tu réponds<br>il / elle répond<br>nous répondons<br>vous répondez<br>ils / elles répondent | j'ai répondu<br>tu as répondu<br>il / elle a répondu<br>nous avons répondu<br>vous avez répondu<br>ils /elles ont répondu | je répondais<br>tu répondais<br>il / elle répondait<br>nous répondions<br>vous répondiez<br>ils / elles répondaient | je répondrai<br>tu répondras<br>il / elle répondra<br>nous répondrons<br>vous répondrez<br>ils / elles répondront | <br>réponds<br><br>répondons<br>répondez |
| **savoir** | je sais<br>tu sais<br>il / elle sait<br>nous savons<br>vous savez<br>ils / elles savent | j'ai su<br>tu as su<br>il / elle a su<br>nous avons su<br>vous avez su<br>ils / elles ont su | je savais<br>tu savais<br>il / elle savait<br>nous savions<br>vous saviez<br>ils / elles savaient | je saurai<br>tu sauras<br>il / elle saura<br>nous saurons<br>vous saurez<br>ils / elles sauront | <br>sache<br><br>sachons<br>sachez |
| **sentir** | je sens<br>tu sens<br>il / elle sent<br>nous sentons<br>vous sentez<br>ils / elles sentent | j'ai senti<br>tu as senti<br>il / elle a senti<br>nous avons senti<br>vous avez senti<br>ils / elles ont senti | je sentais<br>tu sentais<br>il / elle sentait<br>nous sentions<br>vous sentiez<br>ils / elles sentaient | je sentirai<br>tu sentiras<br>il / elle sentira<br>nous sentirons<br>vous sentirez<br>ils / elles sentiront | <br>sens<br><br>sentons<br>sentez |
| **servir** | je sers<br>tu sers<br>il / elle sert<br>nous servons<br>vous servez<br>ils / elles servent | j'ai servi<br>tu as servi<br>il a servi<br>nous avons servi<br>vous avez servi<br>ils / elles ont servi | je servais<br>tu servais<br>il /elle servait<br>nous servions<br>vous serviez<br>ils / elles servaient | je servirai<br>tu serviras<br>il / elle servira<br>nous servirons<br>vous servirez<br>ils / elles serviront | <br>sers<br><br>servons<br>servez |
| **suivre** | je suis<br>tu suis<br>il / elle suit<br>nous suivons<br>vous suivez<br>ils / elles suivent | j'ai suivi<br>tu as suivi<br>il / elle a suivi<br>nous avons suivi<br>vous avez suivi<br>ils / elles ont suivi | je suivais<br>tu suivais<br>il / elle suivait<br>nous suivions<br>vous suiviez<br>ils / elles suivaient | je suivrai<br>tu suivras<br>il / elle suivra<br>nous suivrons<br>vous suivrez<br>ils / elles suivront | <br>suis<br><br>suivons<br>suivez |
| **venir**<br>devenir<br>revenir<br>tenir (auxiliaire avoir)<br>obtenir (auxiliaire avoir) | je viens<br>tu viens<br>il / elle vient<br>nous venons<br>vous venez<br>ils / elles viennent | je suis venu(e)<br>tu es venu(e)<br>il / elle est venu(e)<br>nous sommes venu(e)s<br>vous êtes venu(e)s<br>ils / elles sont venu(e)s | je venais<br>tu venais<br>il / elle venait<br>nous venions<br>vous veniez<br>ils / elles venaient | je viendrai<br>tu viendras<br>il / elle viendra<br>nous viendrons<br>vous viendrez<br>ils / elles viendront | <br>viens<br><br>venons<br>venez |
| **vivre** | je vis<br>tu vis<br>il / elle vit<br>nous vivons<br>vous vivez<br>ils / elles vivent | j'ai vécu<br>tu as vécu<br>il / elle a vécu<br>nous avons vécu<br>vous avez vécu<br>ils / elles ont vécu | je vivais<br>tu vivais<br>il / elle vivait<br>nous vivions<br>vous viviez<br>ils / elles vivaient | je vivrai<br>tu vivras<br>il / elle vivra<br>nous vivrons<br>vous vivrez<br>ils / elles vivront | <br>vis<br><br>vivons<br>vivez |
| **voir** | je vois<br>tu vois<br>il / elle voit<br>nous voyons<br>vous voyez<br>ils / elles voient | j'ai vu<br>tu as vu<br>il / elle a vu<br>nous avons vu<br>vous avez vu<br>ils / elles ont vu | je voyais<br>tu voyais<br>il / elle voyait<br>nous voyions<br>vous voyiez<br>ils / elles voyaient | je verrai<br>tu verras<br>il / elle verra<br>nous verrons<br>vous verrez<br>ils / elles verront | <br>vois<br><br>voyons<br>voyez |
| **vouloir** | je veux<br>tu veux<br>il / elle veut<br>nous voulons<br>vous voulez<br>ils / elles veulent | j'ai voulu<br>tu as voulu<br>il / elle a voulu<br>nous avons voulu<br>vous avez voulu<br>ils / elles ont voulu | je voulais<br>tu voulais<br>il / elle voulait<br>nous voulions<br>vous vouliez<br>ils / elles voulaient | je voudrai<br>tu voudras<br>il / elle voudra<br>nous voudrons<br>vous voudrez<br>ils / elles voudront | <br>veuille<br><br>veuillons<br>veuillez |

# TRANSCRIPTION DES ENREGISTREMENTS

## UNITÉ 1  BOÎTE À OUTILS

**5 Écoutez et complétez.**
– Vous aimez la danse?
– Oh oui, j'adore danser.
– Et la musique?
– Oui, j'aime le jazz.
– Et le rock, vous aimez?
– Non, je déteste le rock.
– Vous détestez le rock ! C'est bizarre !

**3 Est-ce que vous entendez...**
1. Vous aimez la musique?
2. Est-ce que tu aimes le jazz?
3. Est-ce que vous aimez danser?
4. Vous aimez la danse?
5. Et toi, tu aimes la mer?
6. Et vous, vous détestez le rock?
7. Vous adorez la ville.
8. Et la boxe, vous aimez?
9. Tu aimes le tennis.
10. Vous détestez le foot.

**6 J'aime... J'adore...**
– Vous aimez la danse?
– Oh ! Oui, j'adore danser.
– Et la musique?
– J'aime le jazz.
– Et le rock, vous aimez?
– Non, je déteste le rock.
– Vous détestez le rock ! c'est bizarre !

## UNITÉ 2  DÉCOUVERTES

**4 Écoutez et répétez les nombres.**
10 – 10 000 – 8 – 8 000 – 4 – 400 – 3 – 3 000 – 1 – 7 –
700 – 7 000 – 5 – 500 – 5 000 – 6 – 600 – 2 – 2 000 –
9 – 900

**5 Écoutez et écrivez les nombres.**
3 – 4 – 100 – 200 – 6 – 1 000 – 7 – 9 – 900 – 2 – 10 –
5 000 – 1 – 8 – 10 000 – 2 000

### BOÎTE À OUTILS

**3 Écoutez et complétez.**
– Vous vous appelez comment?
– Sophie.
– Vous êtes française?
– Non, je suis suisse.
– Et toi, tu es italienne?
– Non, monsieur, je suis espagnole.
– Et vous, madame, vous êtes suédoise?
– Je ne comprends pas !
– Vous êtes allemande, grecque, canadienne?
– Autrichienne.
– Madame est autrichienne ! C'est très bien.

## UNITÉ 3  DÉCOUVERTES

**11 Écoutez et écrivez les dates.**
le 3 mai – le 1er avril – le 21 juin – le 15 août – le 4 juillet –
le 9 septembre – le 25 décembre – le 18 mars – le 27
janvier – le 11 novembre – le 28 février – le 31 octobre

### BOÎTE À OUTILS

**2 Avoir ou être?**
1. Nous sommes formidables.
2. Vous avez froid.
3. Ils ont chaud.
4. Ils sont magnifiques.
5. Elles ont soif.
6. Elles sont contentes.
7. Tu as 20 ans.
8. J'ai deux enfants.
9. Tu es médecin.

## UNITÉ 4  BOÎTE À OUTILS

**1 Écoutez et écrivez l'heure.**
1. Bonjour, il est sept heures et quart, et il fait beau.
2. – S'il vous plaît, quelle heure est-il?
   – Il est neuf heures moins le quart.
3. Rendez-vous à midi et demie chez Martine. Salut !
4. Mon train arrive à 17 heures 42.
5. Oh ! 11 heures 10. J'ai un rendez-vous. Au revoir.

## UNITÉ 5  BOÎTE À OUTILS

**3 Écoutez et complétez avec quel, quelle, quels, quelles.**
– Pardon, monsieur. C'est pour une enquête.
– Oui?
– Première question : quels sont vos aliments préférés?
– J'aime le poisson, les fruits de mer, j'adore les moules !
– Quelle est votre boisson préférée?
– C'est la bière.
– Quelle bière?
– La bière allemande.
– Quel est votre repas préféré?
– C'est le dîner, mais j'aime le petit déjeuner aussi.
– Vous dînez à quelle heure?
– À sept heures, sept heures et demie.
– Vous avez quel âge?
– Euh !
– Quelle est votre profession?
– Pilote.
– Merci, monsieur. Bonne journée !

## UNITÉ 7  BOÎTE À OUTILS

**5 Écoutez et notez l'ordre d'arrivée des coureurs.**
Le premier, le premier est italien, c'est... Non, le premier est
allemand, c'est Franz Kunze, et Marco Mattoni est
deuxième. Ah ! Et voilà un Français. Jacques Denis arrive
troisième. Le quatrième est aussi français : Gille Delaud est
quatrième. Giuseppe Peretti est cinquième, Léonardo
Mancuso est sixième, Albert Graf est septième. Et le
dernier? Qui est le dernier? François Rivière ou Gerd Müller?
François Rivière est huitième. Et Gerd Müller est dernier.

## UNITÉ 11  BOÎTE À OUTILS

**2 Écoutez et choisissez la bonne réponse.**
1. Je n'habite pas chez mes parents, je vais chez eux
   pendant les vacances.
2. Mon frère et sa femme sont arrivés. Je vais au
   restaurant avec eux.
3. Ma collègue a deux filles et elle parle beaucoup d'elles.
4. Ma sœur est partie à 10h et je suis parti après elle.
5. Jacques n'est pas au chômage. Il y a du travail pour lui.

# LEXIQUE

**Le numéro qui figure à gauche du mot renvoie à l'unité où le mot apparaît pour la première fois.**

*The number to the left of each word refers to the unit in which the word first appears.*

adj : adjectif
adv : adverbe
f : féminin
indéf : indéfini

imp : impersonnel
intr : intransitif
inv : invariable
loc : locution

m : masculin
n : nom
p : pluriel
pr : pronominal

prép : préposition
pron : pronom
tr : transitif
v : verbe

## A

| | | |
|---|---|---|
| 1 | accent, n.m | accent |
| 16 | accident, n.m | accident |
| 10 | accompagner, v.tr | to accompany |
| 14 | accueillir, v.tr | to welcome |
| 7 | acheter, v.tr | to buy |
| 14 | acompte, n.m | deposit |
| 2 | acteur, n.m | actor |
| 1 | activité, n.f | activity |
| 5 | addition, n.f | bill |
| 15 | admiration, n.f | admiration |
| 5 | adolescent, n.m | teenager |
| 1 | adorer, v.tr | to adore |
| 4 | adresse, n.f | address |
| 11 | adulte, n.m | adult |
| 1 | aéroport, n.m | airport |
| 3 | âge, n.m | age |
| 8 | agence, n.f | agency |
| 10 | aider, v.tr | to help |
| 1 | aimer, v.tr | to love, to like |
| 5 | alcool, n.m | alcohol |
| 5 | aliment, n.m | food |
| 2 | allemand, adj | German |
| 4 | aller (à), v.intr | to go to |
| 10 | aller chercher, v | to fetch |
| 8 | aller-retour, n.m | return (ticket) |
| 3 | alors, adv | so, then |
| 15 | alpiniste, n.m | mountaineer |
| 15 | américain, adj | American |
| 3 | ami, n.m | friend |
| 4 | amitiés, n.f.p | very best wishes |
| 8 | amoureux, adj | in love |
| 14 | amuser (s'), v.pr | to have fun |
| 3 | an, n.m, / année, n.f | year |
| 5 | ananas, n.m | pineapple |
| 16 | ancien, adj | old |
| 2 | anglais, adj | English |
| 14 | animal, n.m | animal |
| 16 | anniversaire, n.m | birthday |
| 9 | annonce, n.f | advertisement |
| 16 | apercevoir, v.tr | to notice |
| 4 | appartement, n.m | flat |
| 2 | appeler (s'), v.pr | to be called |
| 12 | apporter, v.tr | to bring |
| 9 | apprendre, v.tr | to learn |
| 6 | après, prép | after |
| 4 | après-midi, n.m | afternoon |
| 3 | architecte, n | architect |
| 7 | argent, n.m | money |
| 15 | arrêt d'autobus, n.m | bus stop |
| 15 | arrêter de (s'), v.pr | to stop (doing sth) |
| 2 | arriver, v.intr | to arrive |
| 15 | art, n.m | art |
| 15 | artiste, n | artist |

| | | |
|---|---|---|
| 14 | ascenseur, n.m | lift |
| 16 | aspect physique, n.m | physical aspect |
| 16 | assassin, n.m | murderer |
| 5 | assiette, n.f | plate |
| 1 | associer, v.tr | to link |
| 10 | atmosphère, n.f | atmosphere |
| 9 | attendre, v.tr | to wait |
| 6 | attention (faire), n.f | (to pay) attention |
| 10 | audition, n.f | audition |
| 10 | augmenter, v.tr | to increase |
| 3 | aussi, adv | also |
| 3 | automne, n.m | autumn |
| 3 | autre, pron | other |
| 15 | autrefois, adv | in the past |
| 2 | autrichien, adj | Austrian |
| 8 | avance (en), loc | early |
| 6 | avant, prép | before |
| 8 | aventure, n.f | adventure |
| 4 | avenue, n.f | avenue |
| 1 | avion, n.m | aeroplane |
| 7 | avis (à mon), n.m | opinion (in my) |

## B

| | | |
|---|---|---|
| 9 | bac (baccalauréat), n.m | 'A' levels |
| 13 | bagages, n.m.p | luggage |
| 14 | baigner (se), v.pr | to go swimming |
| 14 | baignoire, n.f | bath (tub) |
| 6 | baisser, v.tr | to lower |
| 10 | balle, n.f | ball |
| 13 | ballet, n.m | ballet |
| 9 | banlieue, n.f | suburb |
| 9 | basketteur, n.m | basketball player |
| 1 | beau, belle, adj | handsome, beautiful |
| 6 | beaucoup, adv | a lot of |
| 2 | belge, adj | Belgian |
| 13 | béton, n.m | concrete |
| 15 | bicyclette, n.f | bicycle |
| 2 | bien, adv | good, well |
| 9 | bien sûr, loc | of course |
| 1 | bientôt (à), loc | soon (see you) |
| 5 | bière, n.f | beer |
| 8 | billet, n.m | ticket |
| 4 | bise, n.f | love (lit. 'kiss') |
| 11 | bistrot, n.m | café, bar |
| 1 | bizarre, adj | weird |
| 7 | blanc, adj | white |
| 7 | bleu, adj | blue |
| 7 | blond, adj | blond |
| 5 | bœuf, n.m | bullock; beef |

| | | |
|---|---|---|
| 5 | boire, v.tr | to drink |
| 5 | boisson, n.f | drink |
| 5 | bon marché, adv | cheap |
| 3 | bon, adj | good |
| 6 | bouger, v | to move |
| 11 | boulot, n.m | job |
| 7 | boutique, n.f | shop |
| 1 | boxe, n.f | boxing |
| 3 | briller, v.intr | to shine |
| 14 | bruit, n.m | noise |
| 7 | brun, adj | dark(-haired) |
| 4 | bureau, n.m | office |
| 4 | bus, n.m | bus |

## C

| | | |
|---|---|---|
| 7 | cabine, n.f | fitting room |
| 13 | cadeau, n.m | gift |
| 1 | café, n.m | café; coffee |
| 9 | caisse, n.f | cashdesk |
| 2 | caissier, n.m | cashier |
| 8 | calme, n.m, adj | calm |
| 13 | campagne, n.f | countryside |
| 8 | camping, n.m | camping; campsite |
| 2 | canadien, adj | Canadian |
| 11 | cantine, n.f | canteen |
| 8 | car, n.m | coach |
| 15 | carreau, n.m | (window) pane |
| 12 | carrefour, n.m | crossroads |
| 5 | carte, n.f | menu |
| 9 | cause de (à), loc | because of |
| 16 | cave, n.f | cellar |
| 9 | célibataire, adj | single |
| 5 | centre-ville, n.m | town centre |
| 13 | certitude, n.f | certainty |
| 14 | chacun, pron | each one |
| 14 | chalet, n.m | chalet |
| 14 | chambre, n.f | bedroom |
| 2 | champion, n.m | champion |
| 11 | chance, n.f | luck |
| 8 | changer (de train), v.tr | to change (trains) |
| 1 | chanson, n.f | song |
| 10 | chanter, v.tr | to sing |
| 5 | charcuterie, n.f | cooked pork meats |
| 16 | chat, n.m | cat |
| 7 | châtain, adj | brown-haired |
| 4 | château, n.m | castle |
| 3 | chaud, adj | hot |
| 9 | chauffeur (de taxi), n.m | (taxi) driver |
| 13 | chef, n.m | boss |
| 4 | chemin, n.m | way, path |
| 7 | chèque, n.m | cheque |

| | | |
|---|---|---|
| 5 | cher, adj | expensive |
| 2 | chercher, v.tr | to look for |
| 5 | chez, prép | at (sb's place) |
| 2 | chiffre, n.m | figure |
| 7 | choisir, v.tr | to choose |
| 2 | choix, n.m | choice |
| 9 | chômage, n.m | unemployment |
| 1 | cinéma, n.m | cinema |
| 16 | circonstance, n.f | circumstance |
| 12 | circulation, n.f | traffic |
| 9 | circuler, v.intr | to drive, ride, move |
| 10 | cité, n.f | (housing) estate |
| 5 | citron, n.m | lemon |
| 2 | classement, n.m | placing |
| 1 | classer, v.tr | to group together |
| 13 | clé, n.f | key |
| 5 | client, n.m | customer |
| 16 | coffre, n.m | car boot |
| 14 | coin, n.m | corner |
| 16 | collectionneur, n.m | collector |
| 9 | collège, n.m | middle school |
| 3 | collègue, n.m | colleague |
| 14 | colonie de vacances, n.f | holiday camp |
| 5 | commander, v.tr | to order |
| 13 | comme, adv | as |
| 9 | communication, n.f | communications |
| 10 | compagnie d'assurances, n.f | insurance company |
| 13 | compliment, n.m | compliment |
| 2 | comprendre, v.tr | to understand |
| 6 | comprimé, n.m | tablet |
| 8 | concert, n.m | concert |
| 11 | concours, n.m | competition |
| 9 | concurrent, n.m | competitor |
| 9 | conduire, v.tr | to drive |
| 1 | conférence, n.f | conference; lecture |
| 10 | confiance, n.f | trust, confidence |
| 14 | confirmer, v.tr | to confirm |
| 5 | confiture, n.f | jam |
| 3 | connaître, v.tr | to know |
| 10 | conseiller, n.m | councillor |
| 10 | construire, v.tr | to build |
| 6 | consulter, v.tr | to consult |
| 10 | contacter, v.tr | to contact |
| 3 | content, adj | happy |
| 1 | continuer, v.tr | to continue |
| 11 | conversation, n.f | conversation |
| 9 | copain, n | pal, chum |
| 2 | coréen, adj | Korean |
| 6 | corps humain, n.m | human body |
| 8 | correspondance, n.f | connection |
| 16 | coucher (se), v.pr | to go to bed |
| 7 | couleur, n.f | colour |
| 3 | couple, n.m | couple |
| 10 | courage, n.m | willpower |
| 12 | coureur, n.m | runner |
| 16 | courir, v. | to run |
| 1 | courrier, n.m | mail |
| 8 | cours, n.m.p | lesson |
| 10 | courses, n.f | shopping |
| 7 | court, adj | short |
| 5 | couteau, n.m | knife |
| 7 | coûter, v.intr | to cost |
| 15 | coutume, n.f | custom |
| 9 | créer, v.tr | to create, set up |

| | | |
|---|---|---|
| 16 | crier, v.intr | to shout (out) |
| 16 | croire, v.tr | to believe |
| 8 | croisière, n.f | cruise |
| 5 | crudités, n.f.p | mixed salad |
| 5 | cuillère, n.f | spoon |
| 10 | cuisine, n.f | cooking; kitchen |
| 2 | cuisinier, n.m | cook |
| 10 | culture, n.f | culture |
| 13 | curieux, adj | curious |
| 9 | cycliste, n.f | cyclist |

## D

| | | |
|---|---|---|
| 7 | d'accord (être), loc | to agree |
| 9 | d'accord! | O K ! |
| 15 | dangereux, adj | dangerous |
| 1 | danser, v.intr | to dance |
| 3 | date, n.f | date |
| 15 | découvrir, v.intr | to discover |
| 3 | degré, n.m | degree |
| 9 | déjà, adv | already |
| 5 | déjeuner, v | lunch (to have) |
| 12 | demain, adv | tomorrow |
| 4 | demander, v.tr | to ask |
| 8 | départ, n.m | departure |
| 10 | dépenser, v.tr | to spend |
| 9 | depuis, prép | for, since |
| 14 | déranger, v.tr | to disturb |
| 8 | dernier, adj | last |
| 8 | descendre, v.intr | to get off |
| 12 | désolé, adj | sorry |
| 5 | dessert, n.m | dessert |
| 14 | dessin, n.m | drawing |
| 1 | détester, v.tr | to detest |
| 12 | développer, v.tr | to develop |
| 4 | devoir, n.m, v | homework; must (vb) |
| 10 | difficulté, n.f | difficulty |
| 10 | diminuer, v.intr | to reduce |
| 5 | dîner, n.m, v | dinner; to dine |
| 6 | dire, v.tr | to say, to tell |
| 8 | direct, adj | non-stop |
| 12 | directeur, n.m | manager, director |
| 15 | direction, n.f | direction |
| 11 | discuter, v.intr | to discuss |
| 11 | disparaître, v.intr | to disappear |
| 12 | disposition (mettre à la), n.f | (to put at one's) disposal |
| 15 | distraire (se), v.pr | to amuse o.s. |
| 3 | divorcer, v.intr | to get divorced |
| 4 | donner, v.tr | to give |
| 8 | dormir, v.intr | to sleep |
| 4 | droite (à), loc | (on the) right |
| 14 | durer, v.intr | to last |

## E

| | | |
|---|---|---|
| 5 | eau, n.f | water |
| 1 | école, n.f | school |
| 9 | économique, adj | economical |
| 3 | économiste, n.m | economist |
| 1 | écouter, v.tr | to listen to |
| 1 | écrire, v.tr | to write |
| 12 | électricité, n.f | electricity |
| 11 | élève, n. | pupil |

| | | |
|---|---|---|
| 9 | embouteillage, n.m | traffic jam |
| 10 | emploi du temps, n.m | schedule |
| 9 | emploi, n.m | job |
| 8 | employé, n.m | employee |
| 15 | employer, v.tr | to employ, use |
| 3 | enchanté, adj | delighted |
| 15 | encore, adv | still |
| 15 | énerver (s'), v.pr | to get annoyed |
| 3 | enfant, n.m | child |
| 11 | enfin, adv | lastly |
| 13 | engagement, n.m | engagement |
| 12 | ennuyé, adj | sorry; bored |
| 8 | ennuyeux, adj | boring |
| 5 | enquête, n.f | survey, inquiry |
| 8 | ensuite, adv | then |
| 9 | entendre, v.tr | to hear |
| 7 | entre, prép | between |
| 7 | entrée, n.f | entrance |
| 9 | entreprise, n.f | company |
| 8 | entrer, v.intr | to enter |
| 14 | enveloppe, n.f | envelope |
| 10 | envie de (avoir) | to want (to do sth) |
| 9 | envoyer, v.tr | to send |
| 5 | épinard, n.m | spinach |
| 7 | escalier, n.m | staircase |
| 2 | espagnol, adj | Spanish |
| 7 | espèces (en), n.f.p | (in) cash |
| 7 | essayer, v.tr | to try (on) |
| 3 | est, n.m | east |
| 7 | étage, n.m | floor |
| 3 | été, n.m | summer |
| 6 | étirer (le dos), v.tr | to stretch (one's back) |
| 9 | étranger, n.m, adj | stranger; strange |
| 13 | étudier, v.tr | to study |
| 16 | événement, n.m | event |
| 12 | évoluer, v.intr | to evolve |
| 11 | exagérer, v.tr | to exaggerate |
| 10 | excellent, adj | excellent |
| 8 | excursion, n.f | excursion |
| 12 | excuser (s'), v.pr | to apologize |
| 9 | expérience, n.f | experience |
| 11 | explication, n.f | explanation |
| 8 | exposition, n.f | exhibition |
| 15 | extraordinaire, adj | extraordinary |

## F

| | | |
|---|---|---|
| 2 | fac, faculté, n.f | university |
| 15 | façade, n.f | façade |
| 4 | facile, adj | easy |
| 2 | faire, v.tr | to do, to make |
| 3 | famille, n.f | family |
| 16 | farceur, n.m | joker |
| 6 | fatigué, adj | tired |
| 2 | femme, n.f | woman |
| 16 | fenêtre, n.f | window |
| 4 | festival, n.m | festival |
| 16 | fête foraine, n.f | fun fair |
| 3 | fête, n.f | festival; party |
| 10 | fier, adj | proud |
| 6 | fièvre, n.f | temperature, fever |
| 3 | fille, n.f | daughter; girl |
| 3 | fils, n.m | son |

| | | |
|---|---|---|
| 7 | fin, n.f | end |
| 9 | financier, n.m | financial |
| 9 | formation, n.f | training |
| 6 | forme (être en), n.f | to be in good shape |
| 2 | formidable, adj | fantastic |
| 11 | fort, adj | strong |
| 11 | fou, n.m, adj | mad, crazy |
| 5 | fourchette, n.f | fork |
| 14 | fréquenté, adj | frequented |
| 3 | frère, n.m | brother |
| 3 | froid, n.m, adj | cold |
| 5 | fruit, n.m | fruit |

## G

| | | |
|---|---|---|
| 13 | gagner (sa vie), v.tr | to earn (one's living) |
| 12 | garage, n.m | garage |
| 4 | gauche (à), loc | (on the) left |
| 14 | gendarmerie, n.f | police |
| 15 | gens, n.m | people |
| 4 | gentil, adj | kind |
| 7 | glace, n.f | mirror |
| 2 | goût, n.m | taste |
| 2 | grand,e, adj | big, large |
| 3 | grands-parents, n.m.p | grandparents |
| 6 | grave, adj | serious |
| 2 | grec, grecque, adj | Greek |
| 6 | grippe, n.f | 'flu |
| 16 | gros, adj | fat |
| 13 | guerre, n.f | war |
| 8 | guichet, n.m | ticket office |
| 15 | guide, n.m | guide |
| 6 | gymnastique, n.f | gymnastics |

## H

| | | |
|---|---|---|
| 10 | habiller, v.tr | to dress |
| 14 | habitant, n.m | inhabitant |
| 2 | habiter, v. | to live |
| 16 | habitude, n.f | habit |
| 5 | haricot vert, n.m | French bean |
| 15 | haut (de), adj | high |
| 16 | haut de (en), loc | on top of |
| 15 | hauteur, n.f | height |
| 4 | heure, n.f | hour; o'clock; time |
| 15 | heureusement, adv | fortunately |
| 11 | heureux, adj | happy |
| 6 | hier, adv | yesterday |
| 2 | histoire, n.f | history |
| 3 | hiver, n.m | winter |
| 2 | homme, n.m | man |
| 2 | hôpital, n.m | hospital |
| 8 | horreur, n.f | horror |
| 1 | horrible, adj | horrible |
| 5 | hors d'œuvre, n.m | hors d'œuvre |
| 4 | hôtel, n.m | hotel |
| 15 | humeur, n.f | mood |

## I

| | | |
|---|---|---|
| 8 | ici, adv | here |
| 9 | idée, n.f | idea |
| 16 | identité, n.f | identity |
| 14 | igloo, n.m | igloo |
| 14 | immédiatement, adv | immediately |
| 4 | impasse, n.f | cul-de-sac |
| 10 | important, adj | important |
| 12 | impossible, adj | impossible |
| 08 | inconnu, n.m | stranger |
| 16 | incroyable, adj | incredible |
| 7 | indiquer, v.tr | to show (the way) |
| 2 | infirmier, n | nurse |
| 2 | informaticien, n | computer operator |
| 2 | informatique, n.f | computer science |
| 2 | ingénieur, n | engineer |
| 12 | innover, v.intr | to innovate |
| 11 | inquiet, adj | worried |
| 14 | inquiéter (s'), v.pr | to worry |
| 2 | inscription, n.f | enrolment |
| 14 | installer (s'), v.pr | to settle down |
| 10 | instrument (de musique), n.m | (musical) instrument |
| 12 | intelligent, adj | intelligent |
| 12 | interdire, v.tr | to forbid |
| 9 | intéresser, v.tr | to interest |
| 9 | interroger, v.tr | to interrogate |
| 5 | inviter, v.tr | to invite |
| 2 | italien, adj | Italian |

## J

| | | |
|---|---|---|
| 11 | jaloux, adj | jealous |
| 2 | japonais, adj | Japanese |
| 15 | jardin, n.m | garden |
| 7 | jaune, adj | yellow |
| 10 | jeu, n.m | game |
| 9 | jeune, n, adj | young person; young |
| 7 | joli, adj | pretty |
| 1 | jouer, v.intr | to play; to act |
| 2 | jour, n.m | day |
| 2 | journal, n.m | newspaper |
| 10 | journaliste, n | journalist |
| 2 | journée, n.f | day, daytime |
| 5 | jus de fruit, n.m | fruit juice |

## L

| | | |
|---|---|---|
| 4 | là, adv | there |
| 13 | là-bas, adv | down there |
| 4 | laisser, v.tr | to leave |
| 5 | lait, n.m | milk |
| 7 | large, adj | big, wide |
| 15 | largeur, n.f | width |
| 15 | laveur, n.m | washer |
| 5 | léger, adj | light, low-fat |
| 5 | légume, n.m | vegetable |
| 14 | lendemain, n.m | following day |
| 9 | lettre, n.f | letter |
| 6 | lever, v.tr | to raise |
| 14 | lever (se), v.pr | to get up |
| 13 | libraire, n.m/f | bookseller |
| 4 | libre, adj | free |
| 7 | lieu, n.m | place |
| 5 | ligne, n.f | figure |
| 12 | limiter, v.tr | to limit |
| 1 | lire, v.tr | to read |
| 10 | lit, n.m | bed |
| 10 | livre, n.m | book |
| 12 | loin (de), adv | far (from) |
| 11 | longtemps, adv | long time |
| 15 | longueur, n.f | length |
| 14 | louer, v.tr | to rent |
| 5 | lourd, adj | heavy |
| 16 | lumière, n.f | light |
| 16 | lune, n.f | moon |
| 9 | lycée, n.m | high school |

## M

| | | |
|---|---|---|
| 2 | magasin (grand), n.m | (department) store |
| 1 | magnifique, adj | magnificent |
| 3 | maintenant, adv | now |
| 4 | maison, n.f | house |
| 6 | mal (avoir), n.m | to hurt |
| 6 | malade, n.m, adj | an invalid; sick |
| 14 | malheureusement, adv | unfortunately |
| 5 | manger, v.tr | to eat |
| 13 | manquer, v | to miss |
| 15 | marbre, n.m | marble |
| 15 | marche (d'escalier), n.f | step (in staircase) |
| 1 | marche (à pied), n.f | walking |
| 1 | marcher, v.intr | to walk |
| 3 | mari, n.m | husband |
| 3 | mariage, n.m | marriage |
| 2 | marocain, adj | Moroccan |
| 7 | marron, adj | brown |
| 14 | mathématiques (maths), n.m | mathematics |
| 4 | matin, n.m | morning |
| 3 | mauvais, adj | bad |
| 2 | médecin, n.m | doctor |
| 6 | médicament, n.m | medicine, drug |
| 10 | ménage, n.m | housework |
| 5 | menu, n.m | menu |
| 1 | mer, n.f | sea |
| 3 | mère, n.f | mother |
| 1 | message, n.m | message |
| 15 | mesurer, v.tr | to measure |
| 3 | météo, n.f | (weather) forecast |
| 9 | métier, n.m | profession, job |
| 10 | metteur en scène, n.m | director |
| 7 | mettre, v.tr | to put (on) |
| 5 | midi (à), n.m | (at) midday |
| 5 | mince, adj | slim |
| 7 | mode, n.f | fashion |
| 9 | mois, n.m | month |
| 2 | moment, n.m | moment |
| 15 | monde, n.m | world |
| 14 | moniteur, n.m | instructor |
| 14 | montagne, n.f | mountain |
| 15 | monter, v.tr | to climb |
| 13 | monter (les bagages), v.tr | to bring up (the luggage) |
| 13 | monter (une entreprise), v.tr | to set up (a company) |
| 10 | monter (une pièce), v.tr | to put on (a play) |

| | | |
|---|---|---|
| 15 | monument, n.m | monument |
| 12 | moteur, n.m | engine |
| 5 | moule, n.f | mussel |
| 3 | moyen, adj | average |
| 12 | moyen de transport, n.m | means of transport |
| 3 | moyenne, n.f | average |
| 8 | musée, n.m | museum |
| 2 | musicien, n.m | musician |
| 14 | mystérieux, adj | mysterious |

## N

| | | |
|---|---|---|
| 8 | nager, v.intr | to swim |
| 5 | nappe, n.f | table cloth |
| 6 | natation, n.f | swimming |
| 2 | nationalité, n.f | nationality |
| 14 | nature, n.f | nature |
| 14 | neige, n.f | snow |
| 15 | nettoyer, v.tr | to clean |
| 7 | noir, adj | black |
| 1 | nom, n.m | name |
| 2 | nombre, n.m | number |
| 3 | nord, n.m | north |
| 14 | note (de musique), n.f | note |
| 4 | nouveau, adj | new |
| 4 | nuit, n.f | night |
| 2 | numéro, n.m | number |

## O

| | | |
|---|---|---|
| 15 | objet, n.m | object |
| 10 | occuper, v.tr | to occupy |
| 6 | œil, n | eye |
| 5 | œuf, n.m | egg |
| 12 | office de tourisme, n.m | tourist office |
| 8 | offrir, v.tr | to offer |
| 13 | oncle, n.m | uncle |
| 1 | opéra, n.m | opera |
| 7 | opposé, adj | contrasting; opposite |
| 7 | orange, adj | orange |
| 9 | orchestre, n.m | orchestra, band |
| 2 | ordinateur, n.m | computer |
| 11 | organiser, v.tr | to organize |
| 8 | original, n.m | eccentric person |
| 12 | oublier, v.tr | to forget |
| 3 | ouest, n.m | west |
| 15 | ouvrier, n.m | worker |
| 6 | ouvrir, v.tr | to open |

## P

| | | |
|---|---|---|
| 5 | pain, n.m | bread |
| 8 | palace, n.m | palace |
| 15 | panoramique, adj | panoramic |
| 5 | pardon, n.m | sorry |
| 3 | parent, n.m | parent |
| 7 | parfait, adj | perfect |
| 10 | parfois, adv | sometimes |
| 1 | parfum, n.m | perfume |

| | | |
|---|---|---|
| 12 | parking, n.m | car park |
| 2 | parler, v.tr | to speak |
| 8 | partir, v.intr | to leave |
| 12 | partout, adv | everywhere |
| 9 | passé, n.m | past |
| 7 | passer, v.intr | to spend (time) |
| 15 | passer (se), v.pr | to happen |
| 6 | pâtes, n.f.p | pasta |
| 9 | patron, n.m | boss |
| 5 | pause, n.f | pause |
| 7 | payer, v.tr | to pay |
| 2 | pays, n.m | country |
| 1 | peinture, n.f | painting |
| 8 | pendant, prép | during |
| 16 | péniche, n.f | barge |
| 1 | penser, v.tr/intr | to think |
| 9 | perdre, v.tr | to lose |
| 14 | perdre (se), v.pr | to get lost |
| 3 | père, n.m | father |
| 12 | périphérique, n.m | ring road |
| 15 | permettre, v.tr | to permit |
| 1 | personnage, n.m | person |
| 5 | personne, n.f | person |
| 1 | petit, adj | short, small |
| 5 | petit déjeuner, n.m | breakfast |
| 16 | peur (avoir), n.f | to be afraid |
| 13 | peut-être, adv | perhaps |
| 11 | phénomène, n.m | phenomenon |
| 1 | photo, n.f | photo |
| 10 | pièce (de théâtre), n.f | play |
| 12 | piéton, n.m | pedestrian |
| 12 | piste cyclable, n.f | cycle track |
| 8 | plage, n.f | beach |
| 7 | plaire, v.intr | to please |
| 15 | plaisanter, v.intr | to joke |
| 7 | plaisir, n.m | pleasure |
| 4 | plan, n.m | plan |
| 5 | plat, n.m | dish |
| 3 | pleuvoir, v.imp | to rain |
| 13 | plutôt, adv | rather |
| 7 | pointure, n.f | (shoe) size |
| 6 | poitrine, n.f | chest |
| 16 | police, n.f | police |
| 16 | policier, adj. | police |
| 11 | politique, n.f | politics |
| 12 | polluer, v.tr | to pollute |
| 5 | pomme de terre, n.f | potato |
| 9 | pomme, n.f | apple |
| 12 | pont, n.m | bridge |
| 16 | porte, n.f | door |
| 7 | porter, v.tr | to wear; to carry |
| 2 | portrait, n.m | description |
| 2 | portugais, adj | Portuguese |
| 5 | poulet, n.m | chicken |
| 16 | pousser (un cri), v.tr | to cry out |
| 6 | pouvoir, v | to be able |
| 12 | pratique, adj | practical |
| 6 | pratiquer, v.tr | to practise |
| 1 | préférer, v.tr | to prefer |
| 4 | prendre, v.tr | to take |
| 2 | prénom, n.m | first name |
| 3 | préparer, v.tr | to prepare |
| 4 | près de, prép | near |
| 5 | près de (x kilo), prép | almost (x kilos) |

| | | |
|---|---|---|
| 13 | presque, adv | almost |
| 9 | pressé (être), adj | (to be) in a hurry |
| 10 | preuve, n.f | proof |
| 3 | printemps, n.m | spring |
| 7 | prix, n.m | price |
| 12 | prochain, adj | next |
| 15 | proche, adj | near |
| 2 | profession, n.f | profession |
| 4 | programme, n.m | programme |
| 9 | projet, n.m | project |
| 13 | promenade, n.f | walk |
| 14 | promener (se), v.pr | to go for a walk |
| 14 | propos de (à), loc | on the subject of |
| 5 | proposer, v.tr | to offer |
| 5 | protester, v.intr | to complain |
| 15 | pureté, n.f | purity |
| 14 | pyramide, n.f | pyramid |

## Q

| | | |
|---|---|---|
| 4 | quai, n.m | embankment |
| 7 | qualité, n.f | quality |
| 5 | quantité, n.f | quantity |
| 10 | quartier, n.m | neighbourhood |
| 3 | québécois, adj | from Quebec |
| 16 | queue (faire la), n.f | to queue up |
| 13 | quitter, v.tr | to leave |

## R

| | | |
|---|---|---|
| 10 | raconter, v.tr | to tell |
| 5 | raisin, n.m | grape |
| 15 | rallye, n.m | rally |
| 16 | ramasser, v.tr | to pick up |
| 8 | randonnée (à cheval, à vélo), n.f | ride; riding |
| 9 | rapide, adj | fast |
| 14 | rappeler (se), v.pr | to remember |
| 10 | rapport, n.m (entre 2 choses, 2 personnes) | relationship (between 2 things, 2 people) |
| 15 | rapporter, v.tr | to bring back |
| 3 | rare, adj | rare |
| 7 | rayon, n.m | department |
| 13 | réceptionniste, n | receptionist |
| 12 | recevoir, v.tr | to receive |
| 9 | rechercher, v.tr | to look for |
| U1 | regarder, v.tr | to watch |
| 13 | région, n.f | region |
| 3 | relation, n.f | acquaintance |
| 15 | religion, n.f | religion |
| 14 | remettre, v.tr | to hand (to sb) |
| 3 | rencontrer, v.tr | to meet |
| 4 | rendez-vous, n.m | rendez-vous, appointment |
| 5 | renseignement, n.m | information |
| 6 | rentrer (le ventre), v.tr | to draw in (one's stomach) |
| 5 | repas, n.m | meal |
| 9 | répéter, v.tr | to rehearse; to repeat |
| 13 | répétition, n.f | rehearsal |
| 19 | répondre, v | to answer |

| | | |
|---|---|---|
| 14 | reposer (se), v.pr | to rest |
| 5 | représenter, v.tr | to represent |
| 14 | réserver, v.tr | to reserve |
| 14 | respecter, v.tr | to respect |
| 9 | responsable, n | person in charge |
| 14 | ressembler, v.tr | to resemble |
| 2 | restaurant, n.m | restaurant |
| 6 | rester, v.intr | to stay |
| 8 | retard (en), n.m | late |
| 8 | retour, n.m | return |
| 13 | retourner, v.intr | to return |
| 9 | retrouver, v.tr | to find (again) |
| 10 | réveil, n.m | alarm clock |
| 10 | réveiller, v.tr | to wake up |
| 1 | rêver, v.intr | to dream |
| 8 | revue, n.f | magazine |
| 7 | rez-de-chaussée, n.m | ground floor |
| 11 | rigoler, v.intr | to laugh |
| 5 | riz, n.m | rice |
| 10 | rôle, n.m | role |
| 5 | rôti, n.m | joint, roast |
| 7 | rouge, adj | red |
| 15 | rouille, n.f | rust |
| 12 | rouler, v.intr | to travel |
| 7 | roux, rousse, adj | red-haired |
| 4 | rue, n.f | road |

## S

| | | |
|---|---|---|
| 16 | sac-poubelle, n.m | bin liner |
| 5 | salade verte, n.f | green salad |
| 9 | salaire, n.m | salary |
| 9 | salarié, n.m | employee |
| 5 | salé, adj | savoury |
| 14 | salle de bains, n.f | bathroom |
| 1 | salle, n.f | room |
| 14 | salon, n.m | lounge |
| 6 | santé, n.f | health |
| 14 | sauvage, adj | wild |
| 4 | savoir, v.tr | to know |
| 9 | saxophone, n.m | saxophone |
| 3 | scène, n.f | scene |
| 14 | secouriste, n.m | first-aid worker |
| 4 | secret, n.m | secret |
| 1 | secrétaire, n.f | secretary |
| 14 | séjour (pièce), n.m | living room |
| 3 | semaine, n.f | week |
| 14 | séparé, adj | separate |
| 7 | serré, adj | tight |
| 2 | serveur, n.m | waiter |
| 9 | service, n.m | department |
| 5 | serviette, n.f | napkin |
| 3 | seul, adj | alone |
| 12 | silencieux, adj | silent |
| 11 | simple, adj | simple |
| 10 | situation, n.f | situation |
| 1 | ski, n.m | skiing |
| 3 | sœur, n.f | sister |
| 4 | soir, n.m | evening |
| 3 | soirée, n.f | evening |
| 15 | sol, n.m | ground |
| 1 | soleil, n.m | sun |
| 12 | solution, n.f | solution |
| 10 | sonner, v.intr | to ring |

| | | |
|---|---|---|
| 16 | sorcière, n.f | witch |
| 7 | sortir, v.intr | to go out |
| 6 | souffrir, v.intr | to suffer |
| 6 | sourire, n.m, v | smile ; to smile |
| 7 | sous-sol, n.m | basement |
| 14 | souvenir (se), v.pr | to remember |
| 13 | souvenir (d'enfance), n.m | memory (of one's childhood) |
| 8 | souvent, adv | often |
| 1 | spectacle, n.m | show |
| 5 | sportif, n.m, adj | sportsman; athletic |
| 16 | squelette, n.m | skeleton |
| 9 | stage, n.m | training course |
| 12 | station de métro, n.f | underground station |
| 14 | studio, n.m | studio flat |
| 7 | style, n.m | style |
| 10 | succès, n.m | success |
| 5 | sucré, adj | sweet |
| 3 | sud, n.m | south |
| 2 | suédois, adj | Swedish |
| 2 | suisse, adj | Swiss |
| 16 | suite, n.f | following episode |
| 13 | suivre, v.tr | to follow |
| 13 | sûr, adj | sure |
| 3 | surprise, n.f | surprise |
| 14 | symbole, n.m | symbol |

## T

| | | |
|---|---|---|
| 1 | tableau, n.m | table |
| 7 | taille, n.f | size |
| 13 | tante, n.f | aunt |
| 15 | tard, adv | late |
| 5 | tarte, n.f | pie, tart |
| 6 | tasse, n.f | cup |
| 2 | technicien, n.m | technician |
| 6 | technique, n.f | technique |
| 1 | télévision, n.f, télé | television |
| 3 | téléphoner (à), v.tr | to telephone |
| 3 | temps, n.m | weather |
| 3 | terminer, v.tr | to finish |
| 8 | terminus, n.m | terminus |
| 2 | terrasse, n.f | terrace |
| 6 | tête, n.f | head |
| 5 | thé, n.m | tea |
| 1 | théâtre, n.m | theatre |
| 10 | thème, n.m | theme |
| 11 | timide, adj | shy |
| 10 | toilette (faire sa), n.f | to get washed |
| 5 | tomate, n.f | tomato |
| 11 | tomber, v.intr | to fall |
| 11 | tomber amoureux, v.tr | to fall in love |
| 5 | tonne, n.f | metric ton |
| 2 | toujours, adv | still |
| 4 | tourner, v.tr/intr | to turn |
| 16 | tout à coup, loc | suddenly |
| 5 | tout de suite, loc | immediately |
| 4 | tout droit, loc | straight ahead |
| 10 | tout le temps, loc | all the time |
| 1 | train, n.m | train |
| 16 | train fantôme, n.m | ghost train |
| 10 | traîner, v | to hang around |
| 8 | tranquille, adj | quiet |
| 1 | transport, n.m | transport |

| | | |
|---|---|---|
| 4 | travail, n.m | work |
| 2 | travailler, v.intr | to work |
| 15 | travers (à), loc | through |
| 4 | traverser, v.tr | to cross |
| 8 | troisième âge, n.m | senior citizens |
| 2 | trouver, v.tr | to find |
| 9 | type, n.m | man, chap |

## U

| | | |
|---|---|---|
| 2 | université, n.f | university |
| 2 | usine, n.f | factory |
| 15 | utiliser, v.tr | to use |

## V

| | | |
|---|---|---|
| 8 | vacances, n.f | holidays |
| 10 | vaisselle, n.f | washing up |
| 16 | veille, n.f | day before |
| 1 | vélo, n.m | bicycle |
| 2 | vendeur, n.m | salesman |
| 9 | vendre, v.tr | to sell |
| 3 | venir, v.intr | to come |
| 10 | venir chercher (à la maison), v | to come & fetch (at the house) |
| 9 | vente (service après vente), n.f | sale (after-sales department/service) |
| 11 | verre, n.m | glass |
| 7 | vert, adj | green |
| 7 | vêtement, n.m | article of clothing |
| 2 | vie, n.f | life |
| 16 | vieux, vieille, adj | old |
| 1 | ville, n.f | town, city |
| 5 | vin, n.m | wine |
| 16 | virage, n.m | bend |
| 8 | visiter, v.tr | to visit |
| 12 | vite, adv | quick!; quickly |
| 13 | vivre, v.intr | to live |
| 8 | voie, n.f | railway track |
| 11 | voir, v.tr | to see |
| 3 | voisin, n.m | neighbour |
| 1 | voiture, n.f | car |
| 6 | voix, n.f | voice |
| 4 | vouloir, v.tr | to want |
| 6 | voyage, n.m | trip, journey |
| 1 | voyager, v.intr | to travel |
| 13 | vrai, adj | true |

## Y

| | | |
|---|---|---|
| 5 | yaourt, n.m | yoghurt |

## Z

| | | |
|---|---|---|
| 12 | zone piétonne, n.f | pedestrian precinct |